Oscar Fay Adams

Dear old storytellers by Oscar Fay Adams

Twelve portraits

Oscar Fay Adams

Dear old storytellers by Oscar Fay Adams
Twelve portraits

ISBN/EAN: 9783743331433

Manufactured in Europe, USA, Canada, Australia, Japa

Cover: Foto ©ninafisch / pixelio.de

Manufactured and distributed by brebook publishing software (www.brebook.com)

Oscar Fay Adams

Dear old storytellers by Oscar Fay Adams

HOMER.

(After painting by François Gerard.)

DEAR OLD STORY-TELLERS

BY

OSCAR FAY ADAMS

Author of "Post-Laureate Idyls," and Editor of "Through the Year with the Poets," "Chapters from Jane Austen," etc.

TWELVE PORTRAITS

BOSTON
D LOTHROP COMPANY
WASHINGTON STREET OPPOSITE BROMFIELD

COPYRIGHT, 1889,
BY
D. LOTHROP COMPANY.

Press of
Berwick & Smith,
Boston.

Brother beloved,
I lay this wre...
Forgive their sca...
His love who br...

CONTENTS.

CHAPTER I.
HOMER: TALES AND ROMANCES 9

CHAPTER II.
THE ARABIAN NIGHTS 26

CHAPTER III.
ÆSOP 39

CHAPTER IV.
MOTHER GOOSE 55

CHAPTER V.
CHARLES PERRAULT 74

CHAPTER VI.
THE BROTHERS GRIMM 89

CONTENTS.

CHAPTER VII.

LA FONTAINE, THE GOOD 108

CHAPTER VIII.

EDOUARD RENE LEFEBRE LABOULAYE . . 125

CHAPTER IX.

HANS CHRISTIAN ANDERSEN 143

CHAPTER X.

DAVID DEFOE 164

CHAPTER XI.

LA MOTTE FOUQUE, THE VALIANT . . . 178

CHAPTER XII.

THE AUTHOR OF "PAUL AND VIRGINIA." . . 193

DEAR OLD STORY-TELLERS.

CHAPTER I.

HOMER: TALES AND ROMANCES.

HISTORY and fiction have always been unequal rivals for favor, and where ten men will read history with sincere interest, a hundred will turn from history to fiction with relief.

The more closely history adheres to facts, the less the general reader cares for it. The historical narratives that have been most widely popular have been those of a legendary character. The more unreal, the more romantic the history, the greater its hold upon the average reader.

An inability to separate the false from the true, the romance from the fact, is characteristic of the early chronicles of all nations. The lively imagination of ruder peoples in early times has always invested nearly everything with which they had to do with a veil of romance. Their religious rites, their daily tasks, their pleasures and their pains became mixed with this element of the unreal. Beside the gods and goddesses in whom they believed and whose bodily appearance on earth might be expected at any moment, all nature was by their imagination peopled with myriad forms, more or less human in their attributes, and more or less — but usually less — kindly disposed towards mankind. A firm belief in these existences made a love for the marvelous an universal thing. No hero arose but that half-miraculous powers were ascribed to him. It was not enough that he must be victorious over his fellowmen, he must have slain giants, have vanquished dragons or conquered his enemies by summoning to his aid the mysterious

HOMER.
(Bust in British Museum, London)

powers of earth and air. Homer, the greatest of the ancient story-tellers, when relating the history of the siege of Troy or recounting the wanderings of Ulysses, heightened the interest of his narrations by interweaving into his accounts of the prowess of his heroes tales of the interposition of the gods in their behalf and of their continual and intimate relations with supernal powers. And all the romancers from Homer down have depended more or less upon the supernatural or unreal to deepen the fascination of their tales. In such ways the account of the life of any early hero has become so mixed with the marvelous and the impossible that the very fact of his existence is often rendered a matter of doubt.

With the coming of Christianity many pagan myths became merged into half-comprehended Christian ceremonies and beliefs, and pagan tales and legends of the saints were sometimes strangely blended. In all, however, the element of romance, of the fantastic, of the unreal, is stronger than anything else; because the liking for the romantic is one of the strongest of human emotions. The highest civilization refines this liking, it reduces its power somewhat, but it does not extinguish it.

The Norseman delighted in stories of Thor and Odin and their exploits in the days of his paganism; and when a dim and doubtful Christianity came with Olaf, he transferred to Christian heroes many of the attributes of his pagan gods. The history of the Norsemen is a confused jumble of Thor and Odin, the marvelous deeds of yellow-haired sea-kings and their stormy loves and hates, and when the land grew quieter in the lapse of centuries the tales of these restless days, so full of the romantic and marvelous, never lost, nor have they yet, their power to charm. Mr. William Morris writes in our day such poems of Norse loves and hatreds as "The Lovers of Gudrun" and "Sigurd, the Volsung," and the world reads them with delight.

The Welshman was as romantic as his Norse

HOMER.
(Bust in National Museum, Naples.)

kinsman; and in the *Mabinogion* and other collections of tales he has left us a fantastic mixture of Pagan and Christian romance. Of some of these Welsh heroes we read in Tennyson's *Idyls of the King.*

Many of the Irish and Highland legends have a common source and are quite as wildly romantic as the Norse or Welsh stories. One of the most beautiful of the Irish legends is told in verse in Dr. Joyce's *Deirdrè;* and in Miss Katharine Tynan's *Shamrocks* the story of Diarmuid is finely given. Diarmuid, whose story is related by both Irish and Highland bards, seems to have been a sort of Adonis and Paris combined, and like Adonis was killed by a boar. This legend, common to both nations, could no doubt be traced to the same source as the classical story of Adonis.

A general likeness exists between the romances of European nations, and archæologists have traced a great number of them back to Asiatic or Egyptian sources. Some of our most familiar nursery tales appear in various forms in the romantic literature of many nations, varied in each case to accord with national peculiarities. The story of Cinderella, for example, is given in French, Italian, Arabian and Egyptian versions and is known even among some tribes of North American Indians. The Egyptian as being the earliest, may probably claim to be the original. It is as follows: In the year 670 B. C. the beautiful Princess Rhodope was bathing in the river and had left her garments on the river's brink. The glitter of her jeweled shoes attracted an eagle hovering in the air above her who, swooping down, caught up one of the shoes in his beak and bore it away. Passing over Memphis in his flight the shoe dropped from his beak into the lap of King Psammetichus who was then holding a court of justice. The king, much attracted by the dainty beauty of the shoe, sent forth a royal edict requesting the owner to apply for it in person. As days went by and no applicant appeared messengers were at length sent out who in process of time found the Princess

Rhodope still mourning for her lost shoe. She was soon after brought before the king who married her. In the Italian version, still occasionally acted at carnivals, the outline of the story as just narrated is presented, Italian personages being substituted for Egyptian. The French version places the scene in quite humble life, as we shall see if we read the fairy tales of Charles Perrault of whom we shall hear further on. Ih "The Story of Rhodope," one of the tales in Mr. William Morris's *Earthly Paradise*, the adventure is again told, though one not familiar with the Egyptian version might not perhaps recognize the well-known tale of Cinderella. The theft of the shoe is thus related by Mr. Morris:

"There, as she played, she heard a bird's harsh cry,
And looking to the steep hillside could see
A broad-winged eagle hovering anigh,
And stood to watch his sweeping flight and free,
Dark 'gainst the sky, then turned round leisurely
Unto the bank, and saw a bright red ray
Shoot from a great gem on the sea-thieves' prey.

"Then slowly through the water did she move,
  Down on the changing ripple gazing still,
  As loath to leave it, and once more above
  Her golden head rang out the erne's note shrill,
  Grown nigher now; she turned unto the hill,
  And saw him not, and once again her eyes
  Fell on the strange shoes' jeweled 'broideries.
"And even therewithal a noise of wings
  Flapping, and close at hand — again the cry,
  And then the glitter of those dainty things
  Was gone, as a great mass fell suddenly,
  And rose again, ere Rhodope could try
  To raise her voice, for now she might behold
  Within his claws the gleam of gems and gold.

"Awhile she gazed at him as, circling wide,
  He soared aloft, and for a space could see
  The gold shoe glitter, till the rock-crowned side
  Of the great mountain hid him presently,
  And she 'gan laugh that such a thing should be
  So wrought of fate, for little did she fear
  The lack of their poor wealth, or pinching cheer."

If we look at the stories of later date than these which had their origin in the remoter past we shall find the more unreal the story is, the more romantic, as we say, the greater number of people it interests and the stronger its hold upon popular favor. People like to get away for a time from the every-day atmosphere that surrounds their lives. The easiest way to do this is by reading or listening to some romance which is not closely hemmed in by the facts of familiar existence. As for children the fairy tale or book of adventure is the passport to happiness, so for their elders the romance serves more or less effectually the same purpose. When we read Burns's *Tam O'Shanter* we have left the land of the actual for that of the ideal; a rather grim ideal to be sure, but still an ideal. *Rip Van Winkle* takes us to the same ideal country, so does *Hiawatha*, so do *The Idyls of the King*.

At the close of the last century when the romantic novel had become so absurdly romantic as to create a sort of rebound from its influence in the public taste, well-meaning writers like Miss Edgeworth and Thomas Day, undertook to provide a literature for young people which should deal with facts and have nothing to do with romance. So Mr. Day wrote *Sandford and Merton*, a book which no healthy child ever reads without yawning over it, and Miss Edgeworth and others wrote stories which showed quite as little recognition of the craving for romance so strong in childish hearts. Certain American authors have made the same mistake and have produced books which have ignored this, within certain limits, healthy craving in young minds. It is guidance, not repression, that the romantic instinct needs. Sometimes the ideal assumes the guise of the practical, as in *Robinson Crusoe* and *Swiss Family Robinson*, but in spite of the matter-of-fact style of these tales they are in conception essentially romantic, and it is this that has given them their world-wide fame.

Every age and every nation has its favorite romances, some of which retain their hold on readers but a little while, comparatively speaking, while others are enjoyed by generation after generation. In the Middle Ages the story of *Reynard the Fox* was more popular in Europe

than that of *King Arthur and the Round Table.*
The origin of the tale seems to have been Flemish and the date about 1150. It soon became the common property of the Teutonic nations, and an English version of it was printed by Caxton in 1491.

The stories of the *Arabian Nights' Entertainments*, as we shall have occasion to notice later, did not long remain the property of one people, and the *Fables of Æsop*, which are romances in condensed form, have been the heritage of many centuries and of almost all nations.

Within the present century the greater facilities for travel and for the distribution of literature have made what was once the operation of centuries an affair of but a few months or years — the world-wide dissemination of a popular romance. It has brought to Western readers some of the numberless romances of India, of China, and of Japan, and has carried to Oriental nations a few of the modern tales that Western romancers have told. Now that the romances of all nations stand on the same shelf as those of our own English tongue it is not such a simple thing to be familiar with them all, nor need we attempt it. Those we like we shall read and re-read and merely glance at the others. How long the popular romances of our time will continue to give pleasure no one can tell.

For over a hundred and fifty years *Robinson Crusoe* has never lacked an army of young readers and that army is ever increasing in numbers. The stories told by the Brothers Grimm, and the Hans Andersen tales, are read by a greater number every year.

Will it be thus with Kingsley's *Water Babies?* with Hawthorne's *Wonder Book?* with Lewis Carroll's *Alice in Wonderland?* or with George MacDonald's *At the Back of the North Wind?*

Time only can decide.

Judging by the steadily growing popularity of such books as these it would seem as if they might remain enduring favorites, yet the taste of one generation not unfrequently rejects what its predecessor pronounced good. What books will be forgotten in a few decades and what books will remain perennially fresh for centuries is beyond the power of the keenest critic to foresee.

This much, however, can be safely said: Until human nature becomes a widely different thing from what it now is romances will be written and will be read. The heroes and heroines of the stories which are dear to us may pass utterly from men's memories, the tales which many readers have agreed to consider deathless may be forgotten; but there will then arise new heroes and heroines of romance who will wield as potent a sway over the imaginations of people in future ages as do these of our day. Generations may vanish like shadows in a glass but the love for romance will endure.

> "Last night a mighty poet passed away:
> 'Who now will sing our songs?' men cried at morn.
> Faint hearts, fear not! Somewhere, though far away,
> At that same hour another bard was born."

CHAPTER II.

THE ARABIAN NIGHTS.

"When the breeze of a joyful dawn blew free
   In the silken sail of infancy,
The tide of time flow'd back with me,
The forward-flowing tide of time;
And many a sheeny summer morn,
Adown the Tigris I was borne,
   By Bagdat's shrines of fretted gold,
   High-walled gardens green and old.
True Mussulman was I and sworn,
   For it was in the golden prime
     Of good Haroun Alraschid."

A CHILDHOOD that had never known the *Arabian Nights*, that had heard not of "good Haroun Alraschid," which was never lighted by the rays from the wonderful lamp of Aladdin, and to which the adventures of Sindbad were unfamiliar, would be a strangely incomplete one, or so, at least, it would seem to us now.

Yet to the English-speaking world these delightful Arabic tales have not been generally known till within the last hundred years. Carmaralzaman and Badoura, Zobeide and the three calenders, Noureddin Ali and Bedreddin Hassan are as familiar names to us as those of Crusoe and Friday; but while our great-great-grandparents in their childhood knew, and probably heartily detested, Sandford and Merton, of Ali Baba and the Forty Thieves they probably never so much as dreamed.

The passionate love of marvelous stories so strongly characteristic of Oriental peoples is not wholly easy for us to fully appreciate, fond as we Western folk are of fiction. To the Oriental the story-teller is journalist, novelist, dramatist and teacher in one. In the coffee-houses of Cairo, the tent of the Bedouin, or in the palaces of Bagdad, the professional story-teller is always welcomed.

"In mosque and square and gay bazaar"
the teller of stories can always find eager and attentive listeners. The love for wonderful tales is common to all ranks and it is in perfect keeping with Eastern nature that Shahriyar the king of Samarcand should be as well entertained by the marvelous stories narrated by Scheherazáde as any slave in his palace would have been.

To the few students of Oriental languages two centuries ago many of the tales now included in what we usually call *The Arabian Nights* were more or less familiar; but a translation of a number of them into French by M. Galland, in 1704, first brought them to the general notice of Western readers. A translation of M. Galland's collection into English was afterwards made, and, although it was felt by scholars to be imperfect as well as inaccurate, it became extremely popular. English translations from the Arabic were made from time to time,* the best of which was that by Edward

---
* Foster, 1802; Beaumont, 1810; Scott, 1811; Lambe, 1826.

William Lane in 1839. In this work the translator has aimed to represent the original as faithfully as possible and to give a truthful and entertaining picture of Arabic customs and manners.

M. Galland's version is never dull, but it contains almost as much of the translator as of its Arabic original, while Mr. Lane's translation in addition to being entertaining has the merit of being much nearer to the original.

About the origin of the *Arabian Nights' Entertainments* a great deal of controversy has been raised; but with this we need not concern ourselves. That they are of comparatively modern date may, however, be looked upon as settled, as well as the fact of their Arabic authorship.

Coffee, tobacco and fire-arms not being mentioned in the Tales, it has been argued that they were written before these came into general use, and Mr. Lane places the year 1530 as an approximate date: Haroun Alraschid, the centre of so many of the Tales, was contemporary with

Charlemagne, and with him Arabic magnificence seems to have reached its highest point. But the best authorities consider the stories to have been written at a considerably later period than the time of Haroun.

About the year 1300 a Sultan of Egypt issued an order compelling all Christians to wear blue turbans, and all the Jews yellow turbans, instead of white which the Moslems wore. In the tale called "The History of the Young King of the Black Isles" his people are transformed into fishes, yellow, red, white and blue. The red were the fire-worshipers, the white, Moslems, the blue, Christians, and the yellow, Jews; and from this it has been argued that the date of this tale at least must be subsequent to the beginning of the fourteenth century.

The interest of the tales themselves is very little affected by the question when they were written; but as pictures of Eastern life their historical value is of course largely dependent upon the date of their composition. Judging

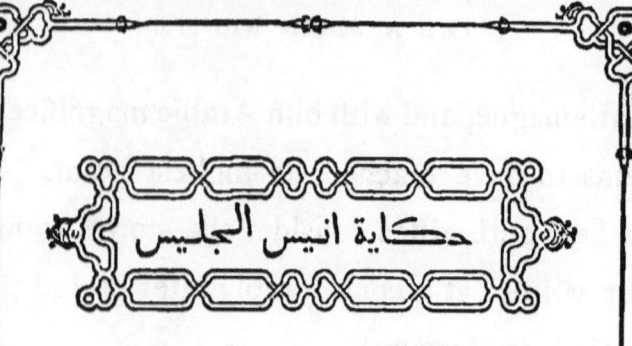

حكاية انيس الجليس

قالت شهرزاد وليست قصة الاحدب باعجب من
قصة الوزيرين التي فيها ذكر انيس الجليس قال الملك
وما حكاية الوزيرين قالت بلغني ايها الملك السعيد أنه
كان بالبصرة ملك من الملوك يحب الفقراء والصعاليك
ويرفق بالرعية ويهب من ماله لمن يؤمن بمحمد صلى الله
عليه وسلم وهو كما قال فيه بعض واصفيه

جَعَلَ القَنَا اقلَامَــهُ وطُرُوسَــهُ
مُهَجَ العُدَى ورأى المِداد دِمَاءها
واظُنَّ أنَّ الاخَذَبِينَ لِـذا رأوا
أنْ أُجَعِلُوا خَطِيَّةً أسمَاءها

وكان يقال لهذا الملك محمد بن سليمان الزيني وكان له
وزيران احدهما يقال له المعين بن ساوى والثاني يقال له
الفضل بن خاقان وكان الفضل بن خاقان اكرم اهل زمانه

A PAGE OF ARABIC.

(Fac-simile of the opening of the story of Evis El-Djelis, "The History of the Beautiful Persian," from "The Arabian Nights.")

from many of the details in the stories they seem to have been written in Cairo, and doubtless a large number of them had been related by Eastern story-tellers to eager listeners in palace-court and street-bazaar long before they were put into writing. Some of them show a Hindoo origin, and others are distinctively Persian; but all seem to have been remodeled to suit the tastes and customs of the Arabs who lived in cities.

Whether one or more persons were concerned in their composition and remodeling is something that cannot be accurately known, but quite probably they are the work of one person, as some excellent critics have supposed. With one exception no similar collection of Arabic tales is known to exist, but in Europe during the Middle Ages, collections of stories by one author were very common. Chaucer's *Canterbury Tales* is one of the most noted of these, and Boccaccio's *Decameron* another.

As a picture of the times in which they were

written they are, of course, historically valuable, but they form no part of serious Arabic literature. They correspond in some measure to the lighter novels of our day; not the novels which stir our deepest feelings, but those which aim simply to amuse. That is all the *Arabian Nights' Entertainments* aim to do. They are animated, ingenious and amusing, but they are nothing more.

Compare Homer with these Arabic tales. In Homer our imagination is kindled by the accounts of the heroes of whom he sings; in the *Arabian Nights* our interest is excited by the adventures that happened to certain people about whom personally we care very little. In Homer it is what Achilles, Hector, Paris and the others really were in *themselves* that we care for. Character moves us in the Grecian narrative, adventure in the Arabic. Popular as these tales have been among the Arabic peoples they have never occupied a high position in Arabic literature both by reason of their literary style, which is far from being the best, and because of their general frivolousness. The scholarly Arab would probably think it a sinful waste of time to read them through and would resent having Arabic literature judged by such specimens of it as these.

I have not carelessly called the tales frivolous. They are so because they have little or nothing to say concerning the realities of life. They are sparkling, but they touch the surface of things only. The fancy is aroused, but the feelings are seldom touched. The mind of the Oriental is not a sympathetic mind. To accounts of the most cruel tortures the Arab listens with indifference, and he can inflict suffering without a moment's hesitation. The greatest misfortune he can conceive of is the loss of money or material comforts, and the interest of the greater number of Arabic stories turns upon the lack or the possession of riches and what they can bring. No moral lesson is drawn from events as they occur, either directly or indirectly, simply because the author does not dream of such things as moral consequences. Vice never seems very black to him, nor goodness especially commendable in itself; and of the development and upward growth of human character he has no conception.

To the English-speaking world life means much more than the pursuit of our own individual happiness; it implies a deep sense of our personal accountability for its proper use. Pleasure is the chief object of living to the Oriental, and he is indifferent as to whether his end is attained worthily or otherwise.

We are not to look therefore to the *Arabian Nights* for any direct moral teaching. But there is in these tales an *indirect* moral, unintended by the author, yet which is there nevertheless. And it is this: The pursuit of happiness for purely selfish motives fails in reality to bring it to us. The heroes and heroines of these sparkling stories are never secure in their happiness for any long time. Any sudden turn of adventure may wrest it from them; and they have no strength of character to console them for its loss, or to show them how to rebuild it upon its true basis — a love for others equal at least to their love for themselves. "It is only a poor kind of happiness that can come from thinking very much about ourselves," says George Eliot in *Romola*, but these people of whom the unknown author tells us know no other kind. If Western nations are superior to Oriental peoples it is because their ideals are higher, because their aims are less self-centered. It is indeed true that some noble examples of self-sacrifice and loftiness of motive are chronicled in the Arabian annals; they are however not the rule, but only exceptions.

If we read the *Arabian Nights* for amusement simply, we shall find it delightful. There are no tales in the world quite like these in their brilliancy of invention, gorgeousness of description or ingenuity of adventure. They can never grow stale to young people; for the love of the marvelous is a natural and healthy love in childhood and youth, and these stories meet that natural desire and in a way that no others can do. Later, when a taste for the adventures of genii and magic-workers fades away, the undesigned moral of it all will grow clear to us and we shall see that character is more than material delights, and that no happiness worthy of the name can be hoped for without it.

CHAPTER III.

ÆSOP.

TEACHING by fable is the most ancient method of moral instruction; and allusions to it abound in the early history of all nations. The dullest minds could be reached by an apologue or a parable, and the brightest ones were not offended by this indirect mode of giving advice. Indeed, the fable seems to have been at one period the universal method of appeal to the reason or the conscience. Kings on their thrones were addressed in fables by their courtiers, and subjects were admonished by monarchs by means of skillfully-told apologues. Eastern peoples in particular have delighted in them, both because of their natural love for story-telling and because of the opportunity the fable affords for pithy condensations of wisdom. Unwritten literature is rich with brief, sententious and easily remembered sayings, and the fable offers the best method of preserving them. The early fables of a race were never long, and thus were readily transmitted by word of mouth from one generation to another.

India was the birthplace of the fable in its importance and the greater part of all Oriental apologues can be traced to Indian origin. In fact, with one notable exception probably no collection of fables has been so widely circulated as the one known throughout India as the *Amwári-Sahalí*, or *The Lights of Canopus*. Bídpaí or Pílpaí, the reputed author, was a Brahmin revered throughout India for his wisdom, who became the adviser of the Indian prince Dabschelim, a contemporary of Alexander the Great.

Eastern story-tellers give a very circumstantial account of the manner in which Pílpaí's fables came to be written. Dabschelim, we are told, greatly desiring to leave behind him some

ÆSOP.
(*After the painting by Velasquez.*)

literary monument of his reign which should be more enduring than marble or brass, induced Pílpaí to prepare a work for the instruction of kings which should illustrate the soundest principles of wisdom and morality by amusing tales and anecdotes.

The Brahmin accordingly shut himself up in his study, with one of his disciples for his amanuensis, and remained there composing and dictating for an entire year. At the end of that time the two issued from their retreat and presented the completed volume to Dabschelim who is said to have been quite overwhelmed with joy upon receiving it.

About the middle of the sixth century the manuscripts were translated into Persian, two centuries later into Arabic, and again into Persian in the twelfth century. From this last translation was produced in the fifteenth century the standard Persian version from which our English translations have been made. All Oriental scholars have united in praising these apologues which, as Sir William Jones asserts, "comprise all the wisdom of the Eastern nations." The book has appeared in twenty different languages and it is one of the great classics of Eastern nations.

In the *Lights of Canopus* as in the still more famous collection to which we shall come presently, animals are introduced as the medium of conversation; the Indian fables however are connected by a slender thread of narrative. One of the shortest fables, "The Monkey and the Carpenter," will serve as an illustration of their style:

"It has been related that a Monkey saw a Carpenter sitting on a plank and cutting it, and he had two wedges, one of which he drove down into the crevice of the board so that it might be more easy to cut it and the slip for the stroke of the saw might be opened. When the crevice widened beyond a certain extent, he hammered in another wedge and drew out the former one and in this manner carried on his work. The Monkey was delighted. Suddenly the Carpenter in the midst of labor on an emergency rose up. The Monkey, when he saw the place vacant, at once sat down on the wood and his tail slipped down into the crevice of the wood in that part which had been cut.

The Monkey drew out from the cleft in the wood the foremost wedge before he hammered in the other one. When the wedge was drawn out both sides of the board sprang together and the Monkey's tail remained firmly fixed therein. The poor Monkey, being ill with pain, groaned, saying: 'It is best that every one in the world should mind his own business:

'Whoever does not keep to his own affairs acts very wrongly.

'My business is to gather fruit, not to drive a saw; and my occupation is to disport myself in the woods, not to strike the hatchet or axe.

'Whoever acts thus, such will befall him.'

The Monkey was talking thus to himself when the Carpenter returned and beat him as he deserved, and the affairs of the Monkey through his meddlesomeness ended in his ruin. Hence it has been said:

'Carpentering is not the business of an ape.' "

But far the most noted collection of fables, and the one that has exercised the widest influence, is of Greek origin, and generally attributed to Æsop. Their purpose apparently was to travesty or parody human affairs, and under the disguise of animals gifted with speech and reason every phase of human weakness or virtue was briefly but effectually caricatured.

Several eminent scholars have denied the authorship of Æsop to these fables and have claimed Babrius, who is supposed to have flourished between the times of Augustus and Alexander Severus, as the author. Others have asserted them to be the work of Maximus Planudes, a Byzantine monk of the fourteenth century. The famous Dr. Bentley two hundred years ago wrote much upon this topic, denying Æsop's authorship; and from that time to this the question has been a disputed one. Still the weight of authority inclines in favor of Æsop, and we may without much hesitation consider Æsop as their author.

That they are mainly the work of one person is evident from their similarity of form. Each relates but a single incident and enforces but a single truth. The lesson to be learned is clear and unmistakable. It is certain that if not all by one writer they show in their construction the influence of a single mind whether that mind was Æsop's or not; and simple, short, direct fables are usually spoken of as Æsopian to distinguish them from the long-drawn-out and often mystical apologues of Oriental origin.

The date and place of birth of Æsop are alike uncertain. Cotyæon, a city of Phrygia, is said by Bachet de Mezeriac, a French author of the seventeenth century who wrote a life of Æsop, to have been his birthplace, while a writer of our own day makes him a native of Mesembria in Thrace, and he is supposed to have lived in the sixth century before Christ.

About the personal appearance of Æsop a similar uncertainty exists. The popular conception of him is that of a much deformed and even repulsive-appearing man; an idea derived from a life of him attributed to the same Byzantine monk, Planudes, who was said by some to have been the author of the fables. Other writers, however, have described him differently; and apparently the only point of agreement in the controversy is that he possessed a dark complexion.

It is also as uncertain as the date and place of his birth and his personal appearance, whether Æsop committed his fables to manuscript, or whether they were transmitted through folk-talk, through story-tellers, and through their illustrative use by public speakers — the collection we possess being gathered into form some centuries later. There are allusions to several of the fables in the Greek literature before the Christian era, but the earliest collection now known bears the date of the thirteenth century after Christ. Their brevity, as we have said, the simple, definite action of their drama, the witty conversation of the few actors, the pointedness of the lessons taught, all would tend to render easy their preservation in Æsop's own words, even through many generations. The remarkable ease with which the fables are committed to memory by any one, and the tenacity with which they are remembered, certainly come from a quality and an art inherent in their conception and construction. The universal fitting —

the "patness" so to speak — of the "moral" is another inherent characteristic of the Æsopian fables, so distinguishing and discriminating them from the common stock of fable that the numberless allusions to them and their frequent use as illustrations and enforcements of ethical truth have incorporated them permanently into the great body of general literature.

All writers about Æsop however agree that he was born a slave. We first hear of him as an inhabitant of the island of Samos where his masters were Xanthus and Jadmon. How great their rank we have no means of knowing. All that is now remembered of them is that they were successively the masters of a slave named Æsop. Jadmon recognizing, doubtless, the brilliant qualities of his bondsman, made him a freeman and ere long the slave by birth became the confidant of kings and the equal of philosophers and sages.

In the reputed lifetime of Æsop the court of Crœsus King of Lydia was the most learned then existing. To the capital city of Sardis were attracted many of the wisest men of the time and among these Æsop might have been found, having made his home there from about 570 B. C. by the express invitation of Crœsus.

In conversation with the philosophers whom he met at the Lydian court Æsop seems to have been quite able to hold his own, and Crœsus appears to have esteemed his shrewd and often humorous advice more highly than the elaborate and lengthy counsels of the philosophers.

More than once he was sent by the Lydian king on diplomatic missions to the various Grecian states. On one of these occasions he was at Athens during a period of disaffection on the part of the citizens towards Pisistratus, their ruler, and by his clever invention of the fable of "The Frogs Desiring a King," now one of the best known of the fables, he restored harmony between Pisistratus and his subjects. At another time he showed the Corinthians the folly of being led by impulse in a fable narrating the danger of mob-law.

It was while absent from Sardis on an important political mission that his death is said to have occurred. A solemn embassy had been sent by Crœsus to Delphi, and Æsop was instructed to offer valuable gifts at the shrine of Apollo and to distribute to each citizen four silver minæ. During the negotiations in regard to the distribution differences of opinion arose between Æsop and the Delphians resulting in his refusal to proceed further with the presentation of the gifts in his charge, which he therefore sent back to Crœsus. The Delphians, enraged beyond measure at thus losing a treasure which had been almost in their hands, at once determined upon revenge. In pursuance of this design a gold cup belonging to the temple was hidden by them in the baggage of Æsop's attendants, and after he had gone a short distance from the city he was followed and brought back on a charge of sacrilege.

To allay the fierceness of his enemies, Æsop related a number of his fables, among them that of "The Beetle and the Eagle;" but the Delphians were too wrathfully disposed to be open to reason, and the embassador was condemned to death. This cruel sentence was at once carried into execution and Æsop was thrown from a rocky precipice near Delphi.

Many times in after years must the Delphians have repented of their impolitic haste, for a long series of calamities overtook them soon after which did not end till a fine had been paid to the grandson of Jadmon, the former owner of Æsop. This fine the Delphians voluntarily imposed upon themselves in acknowledgment of their crime, and from this circumstance arose the phrase or proverb "Æsop's blood," used to indicate the certainty of the punishment following a murder.

What action was taken by Crœsus in the matter has not come down to us, but his own misfortunes followed not long after, and history, which is silent as to the avenging of Æsop's wrongs, is voluble as to the sorrows of Crœsus.

Two hundred years after the embassy to Delphi had ended so tragically the Athenians erected a statue to Æsop carved by the skill of Lysippus, one of the greatest sculptors of the time. The statue has long since disappeared and the skill of Lysippus is only a tradition in our day, but the name and work of Æsop are household words; the brief tales of the Samian Slave have not lost their power to charm and instruct in the lapse of more than twenty centuries.

With some few noted exceptions the Romans produced no fables and their literature boasts no such collections of tales as India and Greece.

The most noted mediæval fable or apologue is the well-known *History of Reynard the Fox*. To this work may be traced the origin of many of the fables of the Middle Ages.

Although in modern times the fable has formed part of the literature of all Western nations, it has never assumed the importance it possessed in ancient times, or which it still holds in the estimation of Oriental peoples. The fables of later authors are with one noted exception read mainly by scholars. In 1668 the first six books of the fables of the great French author, La Fontaine, were published, and three years later a second collection. These fables have been the delight of successive generations for two hundred years, and their popularity remains as great as ever. The student reads them for the charm of their style, the philosopher for their keen analyses of life and character, and the schoolboy for the simple delight which the story affords. Editions of La Fontaine's fables are almost innumerable, and they will probably ever remain as they are now, the most popular fables of the Western world.

CHAPTER IV.

MOTHER GOOSE.

NOT the French *Contes de Fées* or *Contes de Ma Mère l' Oye*, but our own American Mother Goose.

By rights she should be called Grandmother Goose, but "of that," as the crab in the fairy tale said after shaking off one of his legs and while he was waiting for another to grow, "of that, more anon." It is difficult to imagine a nursery without a Mother Goose inhabiting it, but English nurseries know her not, or at best as a visitor from America, not as one who belongs there. Yet the children in the English nursery know as much about the well-merited punishment administered to the piper's son, the astounding egotism of Jack Horner, the sad end of the Gotham sages, the perfectly managed domestic economy of the Spratt household, the unpleasant companion of Miss Muffet, the singular adventures of Dr. Foster of Gloucester and the extraordinary elopement of the dish and spoon as do their American cousins. But it is one thing to learn these delightful histories from books called *Nursery Rhymes*, and quite another to have them directly from the lips of Mother Goose herself, as one may say; and here is where American children have the advantage of English children.

Mother Goose was not only an American woman, but a Bostonian into the bargain. At what time the Goose family came to America is unknown. The name was originally Vertigoose, afterwards changed to Vergoose, and finally shortened to Goose. But the first change was long before the Goose family came to Boston. Boston was a little village but thirty years old when we first hear of them as landholders within its borders. Nearly half the land on Washington street between West and Winter streets belonged to them, and so did a large piece of land on Essex, Rowe and Bedford streets. At that time all that part of Boston was open field or pasture-land, and the Vergoose family before that date probably lived in the vicinity of Hanover street or Copp's Hill. Isaac Vergoose himself, the husband of Mother Goose, owned a house and lot on the land which is now the corner of Washington street and Temple Place.

That the family were wealthy, for that period, we are assured; but only one of them achieved anything like fame, and that was Mother Goose herself. But for her the Vergoose family might have lived and died and been gathered to their fathers in the Old Granary Burying Ground without leaving anything but their tombstones to posterity. The cackling of a sacred goose in the temple of Juno is said to have once saved the Capitol of Rome from the Gauls, and so it is that the cackling of this venerated Boston

Goose has preserved the memory of this worthy family to this day.

It would be pleasant to know something about the childhood of Mother Goose, but of that we are not told in any chronicle. We do not even know where Elizabeth Foster was born, in what part of Boston she dwelt, or when she married Mr. Vergoose and thus unwittingly conferred everlasting lustre upon his hitherto respectable but not famous name. Very probably he thought he was bestowing a great favor upon the young Boston girl when he asked her to be his wife and bear his name; he the scion of a wealthy Colonial family still in friendly relations with its somewhat aristocratic kin in Bristol, England, and she, we are quite sure, descended from no such grand ancestry. But we can only imagine his state of mind, for history is as silent on this point as it is on every other connected with Mother Goose till 1715.

Of one thing however we are sure; that she outlived him although the date of his death is nowhere found in any register. So we grope our way in the dark as regards the maiden and married life of Mother Goose till the year 1715 is reached. Then we read in the record of marriages in the City Registrar's office that in "*1715, June 8, was married by Rev. Cotton Mather, Thomas Fleet to Elizabeth Goose.*"

Of Elizabeth we hear little except that she was the eldest daughter of Mother Goose. Of Thomas Fleet, her husband, we hear much more. He was born in England and was a journeyman printer in Bristol. It was there that he first knew of the American Vergoose family through its Bristol relations. During the reign of Queen Anne a certain clergyman of the English Church, Dr. Sacheverell, having incurred the displeasure of the dominant political party was tried for treason before the House of Lords. The affair created great excitement throughout England, even leading to riotous proceedings in some cases. In some of these young Fleet mingled so conspicuously that he afterwards thought it prudent to forsake England for America. Accordingly he packed up his belongings and reached Boston in 1712. Whether he brought with him letters of introduction from the Bristol Vergooses to their American cousins is uncertain; he may very likely have done so, for we know that he very soon became acquainted with the honorable Colonial family of Vergoose with such pleasant results that the dignified Cotton Mather was called upon to unite him in marriage to one of its daughters.

His first child was a son whose advent was no doubt a delight to its parents, while to its Grandmother Goose it was a joy unspeakable. But not unsingable, fortunately for posterity. Mrs. Fleet's own presence in the nursery was barely tolerated by the enthusiastic grandmother who spent her whole time there or in wandering about the house with her grandchild in her arms. It is not improbable that it was when thus employed she first sung that now deathless ditty:

> "Goosey, goosey, gander,
> Where shall I wander!
> Up stairs,
> Down stairs,
> And in my lady's chamber."

Doubtless all this Thomas Fleet would not have objected to; but this was not all — fortunately for us, and for him, as it eventually turned out. Partly to amuse the infant, and more to express her unbounded joy over the fact of its existence, she was continually singing nonsensical songs and rhymes which she had learned in the days of her own youth. Probably this could have been borne had she been a fine singer. But this was exactly what she was not, and she was therefore a thorn in the side of her son-in-law Thomas. What Elizabeth thought we are not told, but quite possibly her feelings were tempered with filial affection and gratitude. Such was not the case with her husband, however, who exhausted every means known to him to induce Mother Goose to stop singing. He ridiculed her in public and in private and with very little effect in either case. He told her that she destroyed the comfort of the whole neighborhood, which was true enough, for the grandmother's voice was heard for a long distance and Fleet was not the only person who wished she might become suddenly dumb. To his expostulations and to those of the neighbors, she only laughed and sang the louder.

At last it occurred to Thomas one day when the sound of his mother-in-law's voice followed him all the way down to his printing house in Pudding Lane, that he might collect these songs and quaint rhymes which Grandmother Goose was so persistently singing, print them and perhaps turn a few nimble sixpences in that way. With this thought in mind, he listened afterwards with more patience to the not very melodious strains that continually sounded in his ears and wrote them down from day to day till he had exhausted the list of the ditties which his mother-in-law knew. To these he added such as he could collect from other sources and soon after published them in book-form with the title: *Songs for the Nursery; or, Mother Goose's Melodies for Children*. On the title page was a rude drawing of a goose with a very long neck and wide open mouth and at the bottom of the page the words: " Printed by T. Fleet, at his printing-house, Pudding Lane, 1719. Price two coppers."*

In all probability Mother Goose had no suspicion of her son-in-law's intention until the book appeared with its derisive title. What she thought when she saw herself thus publicly made sport of we can only guess.†

* This point has been much disputed. According to an ancient account-book preserved among the Hancock Papers in the library of the N. E. Historic and Genealogical Society Daniel Henchman, a colonial bookseller, published in 1719 a volume of *Verses for Children* which by some has been supposed to be identical with Fleet's book. Also, although it is certain that Fleet in 1712 had a printing-house on Pudding Lane, we find a statement in Winsor's *Memorial History of Boston* which tends to discredit the title-page of the traditionary "first edition" of *Songs for the Nursery:*

† " In 1713, he [Fleet] moved his business to a spacious and handsome house in Cornhill where he erected the sign of the *Heart and Crown.* The house served as a home for his family, offices for his book and newspaper printing and for an auction room where, when the labors of his busy day were ended he sold books, household goods, wearing apparel and whatever else was looked for at a country auction. He died in July, 1758, aged 73 years."

John Fleet Eliot, the great-great grandson of Elizabeth (Foster) Goose, writes in 1873 to the *N. E. Historic and Genealogical Register:* "Mother Goose was a plain, honest and industrious woman, of no literary culture, but who devoted herself wholly to her household duties and could never have dreamed of the world-wide renown she was destined to attain."

But at last Thomas Fleet had had his revenge; a profitable revenge since It brought him coppers in plenty, but I fancy it was not so sweet a revenge as he had hoped it would be. After the first few moments of angry surprise Mother Goose resumed her wonted good nature, took the heir of the Pudding Lane Printing-House once more in her arms and sang on as calmly as if nothing had happened. But for all that something *had* happened. Thomas Fleet, with the double purpose of ridiculing his mother-in-law and at the same time making a profitable matter of it, had immortalized her. What other books he may have published few persons care to know; but this one has gone wherever the English language is spoken. We can forgive him his half-malicious joke at the expense of his worthy mother-in-law, who took such excellent care of his boy, as easily as she doubtless did.

SIGN OF FLEET THE PRINTER, PUBLISHER OF FIRST EDITION OF MOTHER GOOSE.

From that day to this the nonsense-jingles between the covers of Thomas Fleet's publication have formed the stock of nursery song and recital. Each ditty is a story complete in itself, and children remember it, as they do not the more abstract and beautiful lullaby. Generally the child is as profound an adept in Mother Goose's works as the nurse or the mother, and sings "Hey diddle diddle" to itself with complete satisfaction, and entertains itself at solitary play by shouting forth

> "Peter, Peter,
> Pumpkin-eater,
> Had a wife and couldn't keep her!
> He shut her in a pumpkin-shell
> And there he kept her very well!"

Very few of the Mother Goose ditties can be called lullabies; there are "Rock-a-by-baby, on the tree top" and "Bye O Baby Bunting." Generally our lullaby consists of variations upon the one stanza, "Bye-O-baby-bye;" and old hymns and common melodies are sung instead of the true sleep-songs. Other nations than the English-speaking races more frequently sing genuine cradle-songs to their nurslings.

As to the babies themselves, however much those of various nationalities may differ in certain respects, in one important matter they are all alike — they all appreciate a noise that has some approach to measure.

The small Laplander nestled among his furs falls asleep to the monotonous drone of a lullaby as quickly as an American baby would do. The dusky little South Sea Islander is soothed by the jingling of pieces of metal as readily as his whiter-skinned cousin by similar nursery music. When great Cæsar was not great Cæsar at all, but only a very small and discontented Cæsar in the nurse's lap it is more than likely that he gave a willing ear to the nurse's song:

> "*Lalla, lalla, lalla,*
> *Aut dormi, aut lacta.*"

It does not sound like much of a lullaby to us, but the small Roman was not critical. Twelve centuries later the infant Italian was often sung to sleep with a cradle-song representing the Virgin Mary hushing the child Jesus.

Here is one stanza of the nine verses which compose it:

"*Dormi, fili, dormi! mater*
Cantat unigenito:
Dormi puer, dormi! pater
Nato clamat parvulo:
Millies tibi laudes canimus
Mille, mille, millies."

George Wither, the friend of Milton, wrote a beautiful "Rocking Hymn" the first stanza of which is as follows :

"Sweet baby, sleep: what ails my dear;
What ails my darling thus to cry?
Be still, my child, and lend thine ear
To hear me sing thy lullaby.
My pretty lamb, forbear to weep;
Be still, my dear; sweet baby, sleep."

An exceedingly popular Spanish lullaby is the following:

"The Baby Child of Mary,
Now cradle he has none;
His father is a carpenter,
And he shall make him one.

The lady good St. Anna,
The lord St. Joachim,
They rock the baby's cradle,
That sleep may come to Him.

> Then sleep thou too, my baby,
> My little heart so dear,
> The Virgin is beside thee,
> The Son of God so near."

Of the many German lullabies none is more popular than the famous one beginning:

> "Sleep, baby, sleep;
> Your father tends the sheep;
> Your mother shakes the branches small,
> Whence happy dreams in showers fall:
> Sleep, baby, sleep."

Here is the opening stanza of a very ancient Danish cradle hymn: "Sleep sweetly, little child; lie quiet and still; as sweetly as the bird in the wood, as the flowers in the meadow. God the Father hath said, 'Angels stand on watch where mine, the little ones, are in bed.'"

A French lullaby sung by the mothers of La Bresse, not far from Lyons, to their babies, begins:

> "*Le poupon voudrait bien dormir ;*
> *Le souin-souin ne veut pas venir.*
> *Souin-souin, vené, vené, vené,*
> *Souin-souin, vené, vené donc !*"

The Finland peasants sing thus to theirs: "Sleep, little field-bird; sleep sweetly, pretty redbreast. God will wake thee when it is time. Sleep is at the door, and says to me, 'Is not there a sweet child here who fain would sleep? a young child wrapped in swaddling clothes, a fair child resting beneath his woollen coverlet?'"

The Italians call lullabies *ninna-nanna*. Here is one which is sung in Logudoro, the middle province of the island of Sardinia:

> "Oh! ninna and anninia!
> Sleep, baby boy;
> Oh! ninna and anninia!
> God give thee joy.
> Oh! ninna and anninia!
> Sweet joy be thine;
> Oh! ninna and anninia!
> Sleep, brother mine.
>
> Sleep, and do not cry,
> Pretty, pretty one,
> Apple of mine eye,
> Danger there is none;
> Sleep, for I am by,
> Mother's darling son.

> Oh! ninna and anninia!
>   Sleep, baby boy;
> Oh! ninna and anninia!
>   God give thee joy.
> Oh! ninna and anninia!
>   Sweet joy be thine;
> On! ninna and anninia!
>   Sleep, brother mine."

A very beautiful lullaby is one which the Roumanian mothers sing:

> "Sleep, my daughter, sleep an hour;
> Mother's darling gilliflower.
> Mother rocks thee, standing near,
> She will wash thee in the clear
> Waters that from fountains run,
> To protect thee from the sun.
>
> Sleep, my darling, sleep an hour;
> Grow thou as the gilliflower.
> As a teardrop* be thou white,
> As a willow tall and slight;
> Gentle as the ringdoves are,
> And be lovely as a star!"

The history of lullabies and cradle songs is a long one and every nation has numberless *ninna-*

---

* The Roumanian name for the lily of the valley.

nanna. Those I have selected are perhaps as characteristic as any and will serve to give some idea of their general character. The greater number of lullabies are the invention of the common people like the rhymes in Mother Goose, but now and then a cradle song written by some true poet has become popularized among these folk songs of the nursery. Not long ago a young poet[*] died in New York City poor and alone, who never had babies of his own to climb about him or to watch while their mother lulled them to rest, but he loved to look at children and one day he wrote one of the most beautiful of modern cradle songs:

> " Sleep, baby, sleep.
> God gave thee smiles to keep,
> And merry eyes will wait
> Thy coming to the gate
> When thou shalt be a man
> With all the world to scan.
>
> Sleep, baby, sleep.
> God gave thee fields to reap

[*] James Berry Bensel.

When harvest time is here,
With sunshine and good cheer.
But first, as thou shalt know,
He gave thee much to sow.
Sleep, baby, sleep.

Sleep, baby, sleep.
God gave thee tears to weep,
But not for now, not now;
Thy sorrow will not bow
In days to come, and flee;
It will abide with thee,
Sleep, baby, sleep."

Isaac Vergoose

AUTOGRAPH OF MOTHER GOOSE'S HUSBAND.

CHAPTER V.

CHARLES PERRAULT.

"THE iniquity of oblivion blindly scattereth her poppy," writes the delightful old physician, Sir Thomas Browne, in a famous passage in Hydriotaphia; and it often happens that the deeds in a man's life which seem to him the most important are exactly the ones that posterity deems least worthy of its attention. It has happened over and over again in the annals of literature that some piece of labored writing respecting which the author has been unduly proud has failed to pass the terrible winnowing of time, while some literary trifle, the sport of his leisure hours, is all that preserves his name in another age. But for one little work upon which he placed but slight value it is more than probable that the great Frenchman, Perrault, would be a name to us of this century and nothing more.

Charles Perrault was born at Paris, January 12, 1628, and was the youngest child of Pierre Perrault, an eminent Parisian barrister of that period. The Perraults seem to have taken an active share in the education of their children and in his *Memoirs* the son writes in regard to this:—

"My mother taught me to read, after which I was sent to the Collège de Beauvais at the age of eight years and a half. My father took the trouble to make me repeat my lessons in the evening, and obliged me to tell him in Latin the substance of these lessons."

A rather trying ordeal for so young a lad. He seems in his schooldays to have been fond of making verses and even more fond of argumentative philosophy. We are told of him that vacation seemed to him just so much time lost; but about this point I am somewhat doubtful. A quarrel with his master resulted in his leaving college but he continued his studies, and with a friend of his own age read continually.

In 1651 he went with two of his friends to Orleans to procure licenses to practice law, fearing the stricter requirements of the law-schools at Paris. Although it was late at night when they arrived the notion seized them that they must be examined that evening. Accordingly they managed to arouse those learned Doctors of the Law who hastily put on their law-gowns over their night-clothes and went into the amphitheatre. A solitary candle flickered on a stand in the great apartment and furnished but a feeble defence against the gloom and shadows of the place. The three doctors seem to have cared more for their fees than for the honor of their profession, and the replies of the young men to the questions put them were approved of although they seem often to have been very wide of the mark. While the examination was going on the valet of the would-be advocates was counting out the amount of the fees, a proceeding which no doubt stimulated the examiners to pronounce a favorable verdict.

In 1654 Pierre Perrault became receiver-general at Paris and made Charles his clerk. Nine years later the younger Perrault became the secretary of Colbert, the Prime Minister of Louis XIV. In the exercise of this office he exerted no little influence upon the mind of Colbert and secondarily upon Louis himself. Perrault was chosen by Colbert Secretary of the French Academy, then numbering but a few men of letters, and through Perrault's influence the Academy of Sciences was established. He was rapidly advanced in the favor of Colbert and being appointed Comptroller-General of the royal buildings he was enabled to procure for his older brother Claude the honor of furnishing the designs for the completion of the Louvre. Among the competing architects were Poussin and Bernini, whose chief work is the famous colonnade of St. Peter at Rome; but the skill and diplomacy of Colbert and Perrault triumphed and to Claude Perrault was committed the important work, the completion of which marks an important era in French architecture. The influence of the younger Perrault was also strong enough to procure for Claude the construction of the Observatory of Paris and the completion of the decorations of La Place du Trŏni. Many of the adornments of the park at Versailles are the work of Claude Perrault whose genius, however, might have languished in obscurity but for the power of his brother Charles, his junior by many years. To Charles Perrault, too, is due the admission of the public to the gardens of the palace of the Tuileries. Even the enlightened Colbert thought they should be kept sacred to the use of royalty, but Perrault felt differently. He was a man of wide sympathies and considered as well as understood something of what was needed by those beneath him in rank and station.

"I am persuaded," he said very simply, but at the same time very beautifully, "that the gardens of kings are so large and spacious only that *all* their children may be able to walk in them."

His feeling in the matter was so strong that he overcame Colbert's opposition, and the king's garden became the garden of the king's people. Colbert perhaps never fully understood his secretary's anxiety on this point and doubtless Perrault's contemporaries considered it an idle if not an unwise proceeding; but it seems to us of this later day to be verily one of those actions of the just which

"Smell sweet and blossom in the dust."

In 1671 Perrault was formally admitted to membership in the French Academy and he contributed materially to the brilliancy and prosperity of that body, into which he introduced from time to time many needful reforms in its management and customs.

The death of Colbert in 1683 closed Perrault's official career and he retired to private life and for a time devoted himself to the education of his sons. The leisure which he may have vainly coveted in his public life was now given to literary pursuits and he produced about this period his *Parallèle des Anciens et des Modernes, Siècle de Louis le Grand, Histoire des Hommes Illustres du Siècle de Louis XIV, Apologie des Femmes* and several lesser works.

The publication of the first two of these resulted in a prolonged literary war between Perrault and his fellow academician, Despréaux, in which the advantage of learning seems to have been on the side of the latter, but in wit and good-nature Perrault was decidedly the superior of his antagonist. How little real enmity Perrault felt in the matter is shown in the general good temper of his replies. After a long period, so long indeed that the two adversaries had almost forgotten the original point at issue and their friends were heartily weary of the dispute a reconciliation was effected greatly to the relief of the literary mind of the period. The dust of this conflict has settled undisturbed for two centuries and the works which occasioned it lie unread and unopened on library shelves. Despréaux is noted for little else than his part in this long-past quarrel and Perrault, instead of being remembered for the works he labored so hard to defend, is honored now for very different reasons. As the author of the *Hommes Illustres* or the *Parallèle* he is interesting only to the literary antiquarian; as the author of the immortal *Contes de Fées* or *Fairy Tales*, his memory should be dear to every child who has trembled over the impending fate of *Red Riding-hood*, laughed over the adventures of the redoubtable *Puss in Boots*, or followed with breathless interest the story of *Cinderella* from the chimney corner to the trying on of the slipper.

It must not be understood that Perrault was the inventor of these famous tales, which in various forms had existed from earliest times, as we have already had occasion to notice in the case of *Cinderella*. But to him is due the glory of giving to these popular legends and nursery tales permanent form. From the vague and variable folk-tales which they had been till his time, they became at his touch the real, living stories which we know. Three of these fairy tales, *Peāu a'Ane Les Souhaits Ridicules*, and the story of Griselidis were written in verse and these are the least meritorious. One of these, *Les Souhaits Ridicules*, or *The Ridiculous Wishes*, contains a moral the application of which is well worth heeding at all times. Briefly its events are as follows: —

"A wood-cutter, tired of his painful life, was one day complaining that cruel heaven had never granted one of his desires, when Jupiter appeared to him and promised to gratify his first three wishes whatever they might be. The delighted man hastened to communicate this good news to his wife, and they agreed that he must not be hasty, but defer his first wish until the morrow. However, seated before a good fire, enjoying the sweets of repose, he thoughtlessly wished for an ell of sausage to accompany the wine he was drinking. Scarcely was the wish expressed when his wife perceived an immensely long sausage meandering towards her from the chimney corner. Vexed with her husband's stupidity, she commenced a violent tirade against him: 'When you might obtain an empire, gold, pearls, rubies and diamonds, is it a *sausage* that you should desire?'

"The husband, though meekly confessing his wrong, was on the verge of wishing himself a *widower*. At last, exasperated by the continued scolding of his wife, he cried: 'Would to heaven, abominable creature, the sausage were hung at the end of thy nose!'

"This prayer was answered. The sausage immediately attached itself to the nose of the irritated wife. This ornament did not add to her beauty, but, hanging before her mouth, it prevented her from speaking with ease, an advantage so great that for a happy moment the husband thought of wishing nothing further. 'I might,' thought he, 'with one leap, become a king; but then, how the queen would look on the throne with a nose an ell long! I must let her decide whether she will be a queen with the horrible nose she now has, or remain a woodman's wife with the one she formally had.'

"Of course she chose the latter. So the poor man did not become a grand potentate, nor fill his purse with gold, too happy to employ his only remaining wish in restoring his wife to her former state."

The prose tales, *La Belle au Bois Dormant, Le Petit Chaperon Rouge, La Barbe-Bleu, Le Chat Botté, Les Fées, Cendrillon, Riquet à la Houppe*, and *Le Petit Poucet* are told in a style which is a model for careless grace and felicity. They were written by him with little thought that they would constitute his greatest claim to remembrance; but such as they are, the amusement of his lighter hours, these delightful little romances are immortal. One of these prose tales, *Les Fées*, may possibly be new to some readers, at least in the manner in which Perrault tells it.

"There was once a widow who had two daughters; the elder resembled her so much in disposition and looks that whoever saw her saw the mother. They were both so disagreeable and proud that no one could live with them. The younger, who was the real portrait of her father as to gentleness and goodness was, besides, one of the most beautiful girls that one could see. As one naturally likes what resembles himself (*loves* his *like*) this mother was exceedingly fond of her elder daughter, and at the same time had a great aversion to the younger and made her eat in the kitchen and work incessantly.

"Among other things, this poor child was obliged to go twice a day, a full half league from the house to get a large pitcher of water. One day when she was at the fountain there came to her a poor woman who begged her for a drink of water.

"'Yes, indeed, my good mother,' said this fair maid; and immediately rinsing her pitcher, she filled it at the clearest part of the fountain and presented it to her, supporting the pitcher that she might drink more easily.

"The good woman, having drunk, said to her : ' You are so handsome, so good and so obliging that I must make you a gift;' for she was a fairy who had taken the form of a poor village woman, in order to see how far the civility of this young girl would go. 'This is my gift to you,' continued the fairy; 'with each word you speak there will come from your mouth a flower, or a precious stone.'

"When the beautiful girl reached home, her mother scolded her for returning so late from the spring.

"' I ask your pardon, my mother,' said the poor girl, 'for having delayed so long'; upon saying these words there came from her mouth two roses, two pearls and two great diamonds.

"What do I see!' said her mother in astonishment; 'I think pearls and diamonds are coming from her mouth. How is this, my daughter?' (This was the first time that she had called her her daughter.) The poor child related all that had happened to her, the words being accompanied by a shower of diamonds.

"'Truly,' said the mother, 'I must send my *daughter* there. Here, Fanchon, see what comes from the mouth of your sister when she speaks; wouldn't you be very glad to have the same gift? You have only to go to the spring for water and when a poor woman asks you for a drink give her some very civilly.'

"'It would be fine to see me going to the spring,' replied the rude girl.

"'You *must* go,' replied the mother, 'and immediately, too.'.

"Fanchon went, taking with her the finest silver flask in the house, but grumbling all the way. She had no sooner reached the spring than she saw emerging from the woods a lady magnificently clothed, who came to her and asked for a drink. It was the same fairy that had appeared to her sister, but who had assumed the manner and the garb of a princess in order to see how far the incivility of this girl would extend.

"'Have I come here,' said the proud creature, 'to give you a drink! I have brought a silver flask expressly to give Madam a drink, have I? I think so indeed! Well! drink from it if you wish.'

"'You are not very civil,' replied the fairy, without becoming angry. 'Since you are so disobliging, this is my gift to you; every time that you speak, a serpent or a toad will come from your mouth.'

"As soon as her mother perceived her, she cried out: Well! my daughter!'

"'Well! my mother!' replied the surly one, throwing out two vipers and two toads.

"'O heavens!' exclaimed her mother, 'what do I see there? It is her sister who is the cause of it. She shall pay for it;' and she ran to beat her but the poor child fled and took refuge in a neighboring forest.

"The king's son, who was returning from the chase, met her and seeing how beautiful she was, asked her what she was doing there all alone and why she was weeping.

"'Alas! sir, my mother has driven me from my home.'

"The king's son, who saw five or six pearls and as many diamonds issuing from her mouth, begged her to tell him the cause of it. Then she related to him her whole adventure. The prince fell in love with her; and, considering that such a gift was worth more than the dowry that any other could bring him, he took her to the palace of his father, where he married her.

"As for her sister, she made herself so detested, that her own mother sent her away, and the unhappy girl after wandering about without finding any one who would receive her, went to die in the corner of a wood."

Perrault died May 16, 1703, regretted by the nation at large. During his life he was the object of much enmity, but even his bitterest opponents never considered him other than an upright, honest man. He must have been a rare man of which an adversary could write thus: —

"He possessed all the qualities which form the good and honest man: he was full of piety, probity and virtue; he was refined, modest, obliging, faithful to all the duties demanded by natural and acquired ties; and, in an important post under one of the greatest ministers which France has ever had and who honored him with his confidence, he never used his favor for his private fortune but always employed it for his friends."

It is pleasant to know that this writer to whom we owe so many delightful hours in childhood was a man in every respect so far above reproach in all the relations of life. Of another great Frenchman, his contemporary, to whom we likewise owe a debt of gratitude, we shall hear a vastly different story. But in the writer Perrault we can honor the man as well.

CHAPTER VI.

THE BROTHERS GRIMM.

THERE is something very attractive to most people in the thought of literary companionship extending over a long period of years, or for a lifetime even, and the names thus linked together have a double claim upon our remembrance. Who ever thinks of Beaumont without Fletcher, of Erckmann apart from Châtrian, of William Howitt and not at the same time of Mary Howitt his wife?

It is thus we think of Jacob Ludwig Karl Grimm and of Wilhelm Karl Grimm his brother. It is not easy, so intimately were they associated in their life-work, to always think of them as two men with separate and distinct individualities; it is rather of one delightful personality that we speak when we name "the brothers Grimm."

There was but a year's difference in their ages, Wilhelm having been born in Hanau, Germany, in 1784, and Jacob a year later, in 1785. Their father was *amtmann* or bailiff of the district, but removed to Steinau when Jacob was about ten years old and, dying soon after, left his family comparatively poor.

When very young Jacob was noted for his precocity. He read with ease when his mates were still involved in the mysteries of the alphabet. The death of his father might have put an end to the education of the brothers but for the kindness of their aunt, Henrietta Philippina Zimmer, who lived at the Electoral Court at Cassel. She invited the boys to Cassel and under her care they prepared for the university at the Lyceum in Cassel. A taste for drawing seems to have been common with the brothers at this time — a taste shared also by a younger brother Emil, who afterwards became a professor of the art. After leaving the Lyceum the brothers studied at the University of Marbourg together and here they came under the instruction of the learned jurist Savigny, whose influence had a marked effect upon them, and it was during this period that they received the first impulse towards linguistic study to which their lives thereafter were largely devoted.

In the winter of 1805 Savigny, who was then in Paris, sent for Jacob Grimm to assist him in his work there. So complimentary an invitation was not to be put by, but Frau Grimm's anxiety about her son's safety was so great that while he was on his way to Paris she could not sleep but was constantly getting up from bed to notice the weather fearing, like the loving German mother that she was, that he might freeze to death in the diligence, or meet with some accident. She did not live to enjoy the fame her sons afterwards attained, but died in 1808, while Jacob was a clerk in the War Department with the wretched salary of one hundred thalers a year.

In July, however, of that year he became the librarian of the King of Westphalia, an office which brought him a handsome salary and leisure to pursue his studies. It must have been a quiet place, this royal library of Westphalia, for no one but the king could take books from it, and his Majesty seldom availed himself of his privilege. Here for five years Jacob lived and studied, much of the time with his brother Wilhelm, until the restoration of the Hessian government put an end to the kingdom of Westphalia. A year or two later he was appointed second librarian in the Electoral library at Cassel and to his great delight a place was also found for Wilhelm in the same library, and here they remained till 1829.

The thirteen years which they spent here were full of hard work for both, but it was labor into which they put their whole souls, and work which none could do as well as they. While Jacob was custodian of the Westphalian library he and his brother had published several books together as

WILHELM KARL GRIMM.

well as separately, mainly in the department of legendary tales and ballads. But it was in 1812 that they published the volumes which have made their names familiar to every German child and to countless children beside in other lands. These were the three volumes of the Children's Tales and Household Tales, the *Kinder-und Hausmärchen*. The stories in these books were gathered from the peasantry in Hesse and Hanau and written down in a style unequaled for simplicity, ease and truthfulness. Many of these tales were told them by the wife of a cow-herd in Niederzwharn, near Cassel, who seems to have been in many respects a most remarkable woman. Her memory appears to have been a perfect mine of folk-lore and she seems to have delighted in relating these tales. Say they:—

"She told her stories thoughtfully, accurately and with wonderful vividness, and evidently had a delight in doing it. First she related them from beginning to end, and then, if required, repeated them more slowly, so that after some practice it was easy to write from her dictation."

Of their own part in the work, that of putting

these tales into permanent form, the brothers tell us: —

"Our first aim in collecting these stories has been exactness and truth. We have added nothing of our own, have embellished no incident or feature of the story, but have given its substance just as we received it. It will of course be understood that the mode of telling and carrying out particular details is due to us, but we have striven to retain everything that we knew to be characteristic, that in this respect also we might leave the collection the many-sidedness of nature."

It is the simple style in which the brothers cast these tales that has invested them with so great a charm, the homely directness which has lost nothing in its translation from the peasant dialects in which they were first heard, to the polished High German tongue.

But the Grimms had something more in mind than simply the collection of a number of curious peasant nursery tales. They believed that in the study of the history of nations the humbler spheres of life must not be disregarded. Before their day history concerned itself very little with the life of the common people. Their existence was not considered to have any bearing upon the nation's life and it is for this reason that we search in vain in the histories written previous to this century for any glimpses of the actual life of the people who form the major part of any nation. Modern history in the main is written from a different stand-point and does not disdain to show us something of the life of the yeoman as well as of that of the rulers and nobles. To this change in the manner of writing history the Grimms were most important contributors, since they were practically the first to recognize the importance of considering the humbler walks of life as an aid in the study of history.

For several years after this the brothers continued to write and publish together and among the works thus produced were *Old German Forests*, a selection of extracts from the Elder Edda, a collection of German legends, and a volume of Irish fairy legends. But the first great work of Jacob Grimm's life was a German grammar, in four large octavo volumes which appeared at intervals from 1819 to 1837. Of this work, which was really a study of the German language, it has been said that it showed to the learned world for the first time what a language is. While this book was in progress he published a profound work on the legal antiquities of Germany which aimed to show how close a relation exists between a nation's law and its manners and customs and its archæology.

While Jacob Grimm was engaged upon themes like these, Wilhelm was equally busy although the books that he published were not of so ambitious a character as those of his brother. One of these, however, a work on the *Heroic Legends of the Germans*, was considered by Jacob to be Wilhelm's masterpiece. The same year in which this appeared, 1829, the brothers received appointments to the University of Göttingen, Jacob as professor and librarian, Wilhelm as assistant librarian. Although they regretted leaving Cassel, the change in many ways was advantageous and the salaries attached to their new positions being liberal they were not subject to pecuniary embarrassments as heretofore.

At Göttingen Jacob lectured often on comparative German grammar and some other topics and Wilhelm, whose style was not unlike his brother's, upon old German literature and the *Niebelungenlied*. Both, it is pleasant to know, were great favorites with the students at the University. The principal work produced by Jacob Grimm at Göttingen was his well-known *German Mythology* in which book he clearly demonstrated that common superstitions and beliefs are often the remains of a nation's earliest religion.

In 1837 certain political events occurred which put an end to the residence of the Grimms in Göttingen. William IV. of England, who was also King of Hanover, having died, the two kingdoms were declared distinct and the Duke of Cumberland, brother to William IV., became the new King of Hanover. The new monarch refusing to recognize the liberal constitution which his brother had given to Hanover, a protest was entered against the act by the University of Göttingen signed by seven of the professors, among whom were the brothers Grimm. The immediate result of this was the removal from office by the king of the seven professors and the order that three of them, Dahlman and Jacob Grimm and Gervinus, should leave the kingdom within three days. The exiled professors were accompanied to the frontiers by the students in a body who resolved not to re-demand the lecture fees which they had paid the professors in advance.

A year later Wilhelm followed Jacob to Cassel where they began jointly to prepare their great German Lexicon, "*Deutsches Wörterbuch,*" the first volume of which appeared in 1852 and the last in 1862. In 1841 the brothers were invited to Berlin as members of the Academy by the King of Prussia, Frederic William IV., and in

JACOB LUDWIG KARL GRIMM.

Berlin the remainder of their lives was mainly spent. Although Wilhelm from this time published a number of minor works his principal labor was given to the great Lexicon, the work upon which in the last seven years of Wilhelm's life was shared equally with his brother. During his life in Berlin Jacob Grimm published a History of the German Language in two large volumes and a number of other works beside working diligently upon the Lexicon with his brother. When one thinks of the amount of work achieved by these two men in the course of their lives it seems as if they could never have known an idle moment, yet Wilhelm devoted only the daytime to study and Jacob would never refuse a visitor at any time.

Nothing seems ever to have marred the harmony which existed between these two. In their early years they roomed together, studied at the same table and even dressed alike, and for a long time after they became men they had their study-chamber in common. Later they occupied study-chambers which joined. Wilhelm was intolerant of interruptions and could work only in silence, while Jacob, who if left to himself would keep at work without intermission, was able to resume his task with perfect ease after any interruption. The marriage of Wilhelm in 1825 did not disturb the intimacy of the brothers, for Jacob became one of his brother's family and Frau Grimm attended to his interests as faithfully as to those of her husband. The brothers possessed their library in common and of this library Jacob was custodian. So familiar was he with his books that he could find any one of them at night without a light, and he delighted to get up and put his hand on some volume for which the others were searching in vain.

Besides their common passion for books they were equally fond of flowers. They had little opportunity to indulge this taste as their life was spent in cities, but in Wilhelm's windows primroses bloomed luxuriantly while in Jacob's were gilliflowers and heliotrope.

It was not until December, 1859, that the earthly end of this beautiful friendship came. Then the long companionship was broken by the death of Wilhelm. On the twentieth of September, 1863, nearly four years later, a short illness closed the life of Jacob, the greatest of the two brothers whose long lives were so full of noble achievement and were such eminent examples of the value of patient industry. The character of the younger brother was the stronger of the two and to him was due the planning and original suggestion of everything which they wrote in common. He combined in himself a delicate poetic sense with the exactness and thoroughness of the scientist, while his devotion to truth was the mainspring of his life. His literary style was unlike that of any writer of his time except that of his brother, whom in originality of thought he much excelled. But the life of both was modeled upon the same plan and the attainments of Wilhelm are inferior in degree only, and not in kind to those of his brother. How complete the harmony and mutual comprehension was may be seen from the dedication of the third volume of Jacob's grammar:

"MY DEAR WILHELM:— When last winter you were so ill, I was obliged to fear that your faithful eyes might perhaps never light upon the pages now before you. I was seated at your table, in your chair, and my mind was filled with inexpressible sadness when I saw with how much order and neatness you had read and extracted from the first volumes of my work. It appeared to me then that I had written it for you alone, and that, if you were taken away from me, I could never proceed any further with its composition. God's mercy has protected us and left you with us, and it is therefore to you in all justice the present volume more especially belongs. It has been said truly, that certain books are written for posterity; but it is nevertheless even more true, that at the same time each work of the kind belongs first of all to the limited circle in which we live, and that that circle alone contains the key to its most intimate sense, which often may remain sealed to all the rest. At any rate, when you read me, you who know exactly my manner, with all its commendable qualities and its defects, I experience more satisfaction than if I were read by a hundred others, who may not comprehend me properly here and there, or to whom my work, in many a part of it, may be a matter of indifference. But as for you, I know that you peruse every portion of my book with the most impartial and most constant interest, and that not only on account of the subject itself, but also for my own sake. May you therefore be fraternally contented with that which I now dedicate to you."

CHAPTER VII.

LA FONTAINE "THE GOOD."

"La Fontaine's Fables are like a basket of strawberries: you begin by taking out the largest and best, but little by little you eat first one, then another, until at last the basket is empty." MADAME DE SÉVIGNE.

READERS of Charles Dickens's *Child's History of England* will readily call to mind the famous chapter relating to Charles II., so often called "The Merry Monarch." In this chapter the writer in a strain of the bitterest irony proceeds to relate many of the most objectionable acts of that royal profligate, applying the adjective "merry" to each of them. The satire is doubtless overdone, for Dickens seldom knew when to draw the line between moderation and excess in passages of this kind, but nevertheless the chapter serves to point with terrible distinctness the frightful mockery of the term when applied to Charles II. True, the king was merry enough, but it was mirth for which his people paid dearly.

But the irony which applies the title "good" to one whose life outraged the social virtues is sharper than that which styles a good-natured, and yet a vindictively cruel king a "merry monarch." In both cases the irony was unconscious. King Charles certainly made merry with his favorites and they did not dream of there being anything incongruous in the title as applied to him. La Fontaine in his life-time was personally known to comparatively few. Long after his death, when he was known to posterity mainly through his *Fables*, he came to be styled "*Le bon La Fontaine*" with perfect sincerity; his readers, who did not trouble themselves to look up the history of his life, doubtless imagining that a man who could write so wisely could hardly be other than "good."

Let us glance at his career and judge for ourselves how far he merits the title which seems almost to put him into the calendar with the saints.

Jean de La Fontaine was born July 8, 1621, at Château-Thierry in Champagne, France. His early education was obtained at a small village school and later at Rheims, a town of which he often spoke fondly in later years. At nineteen he was sent to the seminary of Saint Magloire to study for the priesthood at the suggestion of one of the canons of Soissons who fancied he saw in the young man an inclination to that profession. But his indolent nature rebelled against the rigor of seminary rules and at the end of eighteen months he returned home. It was no doubt a fortunate decision on his part, for it is not easy to see how one of La Fontaine's temperament and disposition could have reflected any honor upon the calling of a priest. While it is of course possible that he might in this profession have led an upright, helpful life and

JEAN DE LA FONTAINE.

been "an ensample of godly living" to his parishioners, the weight of probability is much against such a supposition.

When he was twenty-two his father, who was government Inspector of the Woods and Forests, relinquished this office to his son whom he married soon after to Marie Héricart, a young woman of great beauty, and, as was proved later, of much sharpness of temper. It does not appear that La Fontaine desired either the office or the wife, but his habitual indolence led him to submit to being guided rather than be at the trouble of remonstrating or of making an independent choice. Knowing this we are not surprised to read that his Inspectorship, which he held for twenty years, was constantly neglected by him, and that his marriage proved anything but a blessing. After some time he and his wife were separated by mutual consent, but he continued to communicate with her by letters at intervals.

The elder La Fontaine had all his life been

given to verse-making and he vainly tried to induce his son to follow in the same path. What example and precept, however, failed to do, was accomplished at last by accident. Dining with some military friends at Château-Thierry, an officer present recited an ode of Malherbe. La Fontaine listened to the recitation silent with admiration, and on returning home he set himself to committing to memory the whole of the volume which contained the ode, and thereafter devoted himself to original versification.

In 1665 his first work of importance appeared, the *Contes et Nouvelles en Vers*. No reputable author of the present day would venture to publish a book of the character of this one, which while brilliant was at the same time exceedingly gross. However, it was thoroughly in keeping with the taste of the age and this fact must be borne in mind ere we condemn too severely its author. Nothing can be more intolerant than to judge the character of a man of an earlier century by the moral standards of our own time. Until the present century a grossness and freedom of speech was tolerated in common conversation to an extent that we cannot now comprehend. People of irreproachable morals indulged in what would at this time be called extreme indelicacy of expression, with very little idea of there being anything reprehensible in the practice.

In 1667 La Fontaine published a second collection of *Contes* and in 1671 a third. Twenty-one years after the appearance of this third series La Fontaine fell suddenly and dangerously ill. All his life up to this time had been a career of pleasure undisturbed by any serious thought of what was to come of it all. In an age of speculation and philosophic inquiry he had remained untouched by its spirit. He had literally taken no thought for the morrow either from the standpoint of faith or of scepticism. He had lived as the gay world immediately around him lived, and like the nominal Christians of his time he turned to religion only when pleasure had no more in store for him. During his illness he was visited by Father Poujet, vicar of the parish of St. Roch in Paris, who undertook to bring back this careless butterfly soul to the Church. Poujet was most assiduous in his visits, and La Fontaine, always intellectually indolent, was at this time when enfeebled by illness little disposed to question seriously concerning points of faith. The result is easy to foresee. La Fontaine was reconciled to the Church. The few objections raised by the poet were successfully met by the priest who as a condition of the Church's forgiveness required that La Fontaine should make an authentic recantation of the *Contes* and a formal expression of his sorrow for having written so immoral a book.

It is by no means probable that the poet at all realized the force of Poujet's objections; it is doubtful if his mind was so constituted that he could do so. He yielded nevertheless, and even burnt an unpublished comedy of his own to which his confessor objected and this, which he esteemed his best work, was no light sacrifice for him to make.

To La Fontaine's greatest work, the *Fables* which bear his name, Father Poujet could fortunately bring no objection. The year 1668 was the date of the publication of the first of these in a volume dedicated to the Dauphin and entitled *Fables Choisies Mises en Vers*. La Fontaine at first seems to have limited himself to versions of the Æsopian fables as rendered in Latin verse by Phædrus, who flourished in the time of Tiberius; but later he drew from the old French fables of Marie de France composed in the thirteenth century, as well as from subsequent narrators of fables.

These fables met with speedy recognition, and for two hundred years and more have never been named but with praise. Says a recent writer: —

"The fables have long since passed out of the region of criticism; where copies or imitations, they are held by the assent of all men to have surpassed their originals, and where original, they take the foremost rank amongst the gems of European literature. The profoundness and at the same time their infinite simplicity, are consigned unalterably to the author's credit in his contrasting, but equally undisputed titles of 'The Inspired Innocent' and 'The Solomon of Poets.'"

A period of ten years elapsed between the appearance of the first and second collections of *Fables*, the latter being published in 1678-79. As in the first collection, a number of the fables were dedicated to individuals and many of them were inspired by contemporary events. At this time the poet was at the height of his reputation and his popularity, except at court, was very great. For the composer Lully he wrote about this period the opera of *Daphne* which was the beginning of his efforts in dramatic composition.

Doubtless few poets of the present day would feel moved to celebrate in verse the virtues of any medicinal agent, least of all that of quinine, but at the suggestion of the Duchesse de Bouillon La Fontaine wrote a poem of two cantos on the subject, called *Le Quinquina*. The poem was published in 1682, soon after the use of quinine had become popular. Thirty years before the chief of the Jesuits in America had carried powdered quinine to Rome where it was sold for a long time at most exorbitant prices as the *poudre des pères* or *poudre des Jesuites*. An Englishman named Talbot in 1679 introduced a mode of infusing it in wine, and in France it then became known as *le remède anglais*.

In 1683 he obtained the great prize of literary ambition in France — a seat in the French Academy — though not without some opposition in the course of which the immorality of the *Contes* was repeatedly urged as a reason for his non-admission.

After his recovery from the illness before mentioned he gathered into a volume the fables he had composed in the years following the issue of the second collection of apologues, and also wrote several hymns. But he was now past seventy years old and there was little more for him to do. His slender remaining strength was devoted to the practices of religion and it was found after his death that the hair shirt of the austere penitent had long been worn next his skin. His death occurred on April 13, 1695, at the house of one of his friends, M. d'Hervart, and he was buried beside his friend Molière in the parish churchyard of St. Joseph.

In some respects La Fontaine remained a child to the hour of his death. He was incapable of taking care of himself in ordinary affairs of life and was always dependent upon one protector or another. He was almost entirely without resentment and the simplicity of his nature presents a refreshing contrast to the duplicity of many of his contemporaries. That in an age when virtue was the exception to the general rule La Fontaine was conspicuous for his violations of moral obligations may be accounted for by the fact that his was a nature which found it difficult to take account of moral distinctions. He seemed to have been born with very clouded moral perceptions, if indeed he can be said to have had in some directions any moral sense at all. His native indolence made vice not only easier to him than virtue, but with his constitutionally perverted sense of right and wrong often made it appear the only natural course to pursue. This does not clear him from blame, for some degree of free agency he certainly possessed, but after all is said that can be urged against him there remains much to his credit. If he were not "good" in the ordinary acception of the term he possessed some desirable attributes of goodness. We read of him that he was "unaffected, truthful and compassionate; he stood firmly by his friend in trouble, and was invariably patient and forgiving." He was capable of strong attachments, and in one very notable instance stood manfully by the friend who had once befriended him, the Minister Fouquet, in the disgrace that befell his former patron, and did much to allay popular indignation against that fallen dignitary.

In society his absent-mindedness became almost a proverb and his manners were very frequently, taciturn, even boorish. In discussions he never listened to his opponents and talked on, hearing only the sound of his own voice. On one occasion in a conversation on dramatic art La Fontaine strongly condemned the custom of stage "asides," saying that nothing could be more absurd than to suppose that an actor could be heard in the gallery and not by people beside him. The discussion became a heated one, and the poet's voice rose high above all the rest. He did not know that all the while Despréaux, one of the company, was incessantly calling him aloud all kinds of names — "La Fontaine is a scoundrel, a blockhead, a calf, an owl," till every one around him was laughing. On his then inquiring what the matter was, Despréaux said: "Here am I calling you the hardest names I can think of and you don't hear me, although I am near enough to touch your elbow; and yet you think it extraordinary that one actor should not be able to hear another who may be ten paces away from him."

One of the most serious indictments against La Fontaine is his neglect of his son. The youth was educated by a friend of La Fontaine's, and from the time of his removal from his father's notice the poet seems to have forgotten him completely, never inquiring for or alluding to him. After the youth's college course was completed a meeting was arranged between the father and son who had not met for nearly six years. The occasion was a dinner, and after it was over La Fontaine's friend asked him what he thought of the young man who had just left them. The poet replied that he seemed modest and quite well informed for his age.

"It is your own son," said his friend.

"Ah, indeed," replied La Fontaine; "I am glad to hear it." Then he suffered the matter to drop as if it were a trifling episode of a pleasant nature which had merely served its turn.

It is a nature full of contradictions — this of the great French fabulist — and it is open to much well-deserved blame, yet there is not a little in it to attract, and in thinking of him it is well to bear in mind the words of his dear friend Maucroix:

"We have been friends for more than fifty years, and I thank God for having allowed the extreme friendship I bore him to continue up to a pretty good old age without interruption or coolness, as I can say that I have ever loved him with affection as much the last day as the first. May God in his mercy, take his soul into his holy rest! His was the sincerest and most candid heart I ever knew. Never any disguise. I do not know if he ever told a lie in his life."

CHAPTER VIII.

EDOUARD RENE LEFEBRE LABOULAYE.

" He who gives to the world one pure and good story, the aim of which is to sow seeds of virtue, a love of right, and that poetic trust in the workings of a wise and good God, he who successfully does all this is a very great man, whose name is to be remembered, who should be thanked and praised, and one — and to such this truth will be more than that title or honor — one of those whom we should upon our bended knees thank God for having made."

EDOUARD LABOULAYE, of whom the above was written, was for more than one reason the French writer best beloved in America of all the people of his time. In the early days of our great Civil War when the final issue appeared doubtful, or the dissolution of the Union seemed impending and foreign nations confidently expected its downfall, there were a few clear-sighted men in England and France who saw deeply enough into the causes of the conflict to understand them and whose active sympathy for the Union never wavered. Foremost among these men in England was John Bright; in France the voice of Edouard Laboulaye rang clearest in our behalf. It is for this that his memory is reverenced by an older generation of Americans; it is as the author of *Abdallah* and the delightful fairy tales called *Les Contes Bleus* that he is beloved by a younger.

He was born in Paris, January 18, 1811, and as in early youth he showed marked talent for disputation he began the study of law and jurisprudence at an early age. Of an enthusiastic temperament, he threw his heart into the pursuit and became known among his fellow students as an indefatigable worker. When but twenty-eight he published a famous legal work, *The Law of Real Property in Europe*, a book which shows in its preparation great research and which gave him a reputation as a scholar. It received the honor of being "crowned," or formally approved by the French Academy. In 1842 he published an *Essay on the Life and Doctrines of Frédéric de Savigny*, the great modern jurist of Germany, and in the following year an elaborate treatise upon the *Civil and Political Condition of Women from the Time of the Romans*. This latter work and a learned essay in 1845 upon the *Criminal Laws of the Romans*, both received prizes from the Academy. Not far from this time he was elected a member of the Academy, and in 1849 he became Professor of Comparative Legislation in the *Collège de France*.

Laboulaye was always an admirer of Anglo-Saxon institutions and it was in consequence of this, no doubt, that he was led to write in 1855 and 1856 his *Political History of the United States*. About this time he translated into French the works of Dr. Channing, and wrote *Studies on Germany and the Slavonian Countries* and an important work on Religious Liberty. Of his books *Paris in America* has been perhaps the most widely read. It appeared in 1863, was speedily translated and hardly a circulating library in this country was then without it. He was gifted with a delightful humor to which he gave full play in this entertaining allegory. In this year he published also a noted work upon the *Limits of the State.* In 1866-67 appeared his *Memoirs of Franklin*, and in 1872 *Political Letters.*

In the midst of the labor given to these grave works, to his daily lectures in the *Collège de France* and to many duties, this busiest of men found time to write in 1859 the beautiful story of *Abdallah*, which fascinates every child who reads it. Hardly less charming are the fairy tales known as *Les Contes Bleus*, which were written in 1862. His *Prince Carriche* which is not so well known as it deserves to be, was given to the world in 1868.

As regards romance, adventures and dramatic actions and endings, many of Laboulaye's fairy tales might be given a place in the *Thou-*

EDOUARD RENE LEFEBRE LABOULAYE.

sand and One Nights Entertainments, while in beauty of style and delicate humor and grace and noble sentiment there is nothing at all in the *Arabian Nights* with which to compare them.

"Yvon and Finette," the first story in *Les Contes Bleus*, opens in this entertaining style:

"Once upon a time there lived in Brittany a noble lord, who was called the Baron Kerver. His manor-house was the most beautiful in the province. It was a great Gothic castle, with a groined roof and walls, covered with carvings that looked, at a distance like a vine climbing an arbor. On the first floor six stained glass balcony windows looked out on each side toward the rising and the setting sun.

"In the morning, when the baron, mounted on his dun mare, went forth into the forest, followed by his tall greyhounds, he saw at each window one of his daughters, with prayer-book in hand, praying for the house of Kerver, and who with their fair curls, blue eyes, and clasped hands, might have been taken for six Madonnas in an azure niche.

"At evening, when the sun declined and the baron returned homeward, after riding round his domains, he perceived from afar, in the windows looking toward the west, six sons, with dark locks and eager gaze, the hope and pride of the family, that might have been taken for six sculptured knights at the portal of a church."

A story with such a delightful beginning as this must surely have as fascinating a sequel. And so it proves. Yvon, the thirteenth child of the Baron Kerver, at the very threshold of his adventures, becomes the servant of an exacting old giant, and but for Finette, the daughter of a fairy and the slave of the giant, is in a fair way never to get beyond the threshold. Finette, however, proves to be a most remarkable young woman and discloses to Yvon many ways of outwitting the old giant. After Finette had provided herself with three golden bullets, two silver ones, and one more of copper, they leave the service of the giant, but it takes all the mysterious power of the silver and copper bullets to get them fairly out of his clutches. After this Yvon falls under the spell of a sorceress and forgets all about Finette who goes through a surprising list of adventures. At one time when a seneschal wished to marry her she fled from him into the stable and hid behind the cow.

"'You shall not escape me, sorceress!' cried the seneschal; and with a grasp like that of Hercules he seized the cow by the tail, and dragged her out of the stable.

"'*Abracadabra!*' cried Finette. 'May the cow's tail hold on, villain, and may you hold on the cow's tail till you both have been around the world together.'"

And behold the cow darted off like lightning, dragging the unhappy seneschal after her. Nothing stopped the two inseparable comrades; they rushed over mountain and valley, crossed marshes, rivers, quagmires and brakes, glided over the seas without sinking, were frozen in Siberia, and scorched in Africa, climbed the Himalayas, descended Mont Blanc, and at length, after thirty-six hours of a journey the like of which had never been seen, both stopped out of breath in the public square of the village. A young woman who can send off a suitor in this style is certainly a person to make herself respected and to inspire beholders with the feeling that she can do pretty much as she likes, and we are quite prepared to hear that she triumphs over all obstacles and by the aid of the last golden bullet reaches Yvon and lives with him happily ever after.

The other tales in *Les Contes Bleus* are written in this happy fluent style; but *Abdallah* is conceived in a graver manner. It is the story of the search for the four-leaved shamrock whose possessor would lack nothing. How the sacred plant was at last won is thus told:

"While Abdallah admired these marvels in silence, an angel descended towards him; not the terrible Azrael, but the messenger of celestial favors, the good and lovely Gabriel. He held in his hand a tiny diamond leaf; but, small as it was, it shed a light that illumined the whole desert. His soul was intoxicated with joy; the son of Yusuf ran to meet the angel. He paused in terror; at his feet was a vast gulf, full of fire and smoke, bridged only by an immense arch made of a blade of steel which was finer than a hair and sharper than a razor.

"The Bedouin was already seized with despair, when he felt himself supported and urged on by an invisible power. Hafiz and Leila were on either side of him. He did not see them; he dared not turn for fear of awaking; but he felt their presence, he heard their soothing words; both supported and carried him along with them. 'In the name of the clement and merciful God!' he cried. At these words, which are the key to Paradise, he was transported like lightning to the other side of the bridge. The angel was there, holding out the mysterious flower. The young man seized it. At last the four-leaved shamrock was his, the ardor of desire was quenched, the veil of the body was lifted, the hour of recompense had struck. Gabriel turned his eyes toward the bottom of the garden, where divine majesty was enthroned. Abdallah's glance followed that of the angel, and the eternal splendor flashed in his face. At this lustre which no eye can endure, he fell with his face to the ground, uttering a loud cry.

"This cry man's ear has never heard, man's voice has never repeated. The delicious joy of the shipwrecked mariner who escapes the fury of the waves, the delight of the bridegroom who presses his beloved for the first time to his heart, the transports of the mother who finds the son for whom she has wept — all the joys of earth are naught but mourning and sorrow to the cry of happiness which rose from the soul of Abdallah."

The works I have named by no means comprise all of Laboulaye's writings. He was a constant contributor to newspapers and periodicals and from time to time put forth pamphlets on various subjects. Among these was one which was almost as popular in the United States as the famous *Paris in America*, and which bore the title *Why the North cannot accept of Separation.* It was a judicious piece of reasoning and did much good.

"No American," writes Mr. John Bigelow, "was probably more convinced than he was that nowhere in this world outside of the United States could be found such durable guarantees to the people, of the right to life, liberty and the pursuit of happiness. He thought it therefore a matter of world-wide concern that our republic should prove its capacity to deal with the enemies of its own household. He was one of the few conspicuous Frenchmen — perhaps beside M. de Tocqueville, it would be difficult to name a third — who knew where the sovereignty of the people began, and he never ceased to deplore the inability of his countrymen to recognize the limitations of the powers of the State as taught by the fathers of the republic."

In 1869 and 1870 when Napoleon III. was laying his plans for the war with Germany he succeeded in attaching to his cause a number of the prominent single-minded patriotic Frenchmen of the time, among whom were such men as Prévost Paradol, Emile Ollivier and Edouard Laboulaye. Trusting in the good faith of the Emperor Laboulaye supported the famous Plebiscite of 1870, and like the others he found his confidence had been misplaced. Like other Frenchmen of that time he believed in the all-conquering power of French armies, and when France was subdued by the armies of the Germans, and a humiliating peace followed, it not unnaturally filled his soul with bitterness. To him Bismarck was always thereafter "the incarnation of vandalic barbarism," and the pleasant relations he had hitherto held with many German literary men were never again imbued with the old-time cordiality. Yet under the Republic his merits received more public recognition than they would have ever gained under the Empire. In 1871 he became a member of the National Assembly, in 1873 a Director of the *Collège de France*, and in 1875 a Senator for life.

Laboulaye sympathized with all important reforms and was an ardent believer in the absolute freedom of education. He was a supporter of the co-operative principles and urged the establishment of great libraries for the working classes. But in spite of his interest in all movements for the improvement of his race he was not in these later years the centre or source of any great public influence. He never became a politician in any but the highest sense. His standards of right were too lofty to allow him ever to stoop to trickery or double dealing of any sort. Perhaps it was for this reason that he failed to achieve the political influence that no doubt he would have enjoyed wielding, but his failure was of that character which is success if we view it aright.

As a lecturer he was greatly admired. His daily lectures in the *Collège de France* lasted one hour and his class-room was always crowded. So eager was the competition for seats that many who came to listen would wait through the hour of the preceding lecturer in order to be sure of hearing Laboulaye. "All sorts and conditions of men" were among his hearers. The roughest men were shoulder to shoulder with scholars and exquisites. In the throng women were often present, many drawn there merely from curiosity, but others from a sincere desire to profit by the lecture. He was a fluent and elegant speaker and his discourses sparkled with humor. Says one American woman who often listened to him in 1869:

"The subject was Montesquieu's Writings. M. Laboulaye held in his hand a volume of the *Esprit des Lois* and read from it, stopping continually to elucidate, or defend sentiments or opinions therein contained. Indeed Montesquieu was only a text from which to preach upon every known subject: religion, politics, manners, literature and art. Now and then the lecturer would condescend to launch a satire against the airy nothingness of a lady's bonnet, the glazed hat of a Paris coachman, the demolitions of Haussmann — in short, he touched upon many a subject never dreamed of in Montesquieu's philosophy. No lecture ever passed without some allusion to our country in glaring and flattering contrast to every other. . . It did not surprise us to learn that the Emperor had forbidden M. Laboulaye to lecture any more upon American politics at the *Collège de France*. The conclusions of the audience was too quickly drawn, and the applause undisguised, but it will make no difference with Laboulaye, for he can teach what lessons he chooses from the politics of Otaheite."

It was a cherished hope with him to visit America and lecture in French upon the topics most dear to him, but the political events preceding the Franco-Prussian War compelled him to relinquish the idea and the fitting opportunity never afterwards presented itself to him. Had he carried out his intention there is no doubt that he would have received one of the most cordial welcomes ever accorded to any of his countrymen. Americans owe his memory a debt of gratitude not easily repaid. For years he was an untiring advocate of the best things in American institutions and his strongest efforts were devoted to giving his countrymen an intelligent comprehension of American principles. To his articles and influence is due the fact that the *Journal des Débats*, one of the most powerful journals in France if not in all Europe, took a decided stand in favor of the Union cause during our Civil War.

In person Laboulaye was about five feet seven inches in height, of pleasant manners and generally attractive appearance. His forehead was high and large, and his lips and chin full and prominent, while his small eyes sparkled with humor and kindliness. His dark olive complexion was seen to fullest advantage, for he wore no beard, and his thin brown hair was brushed smoothly upon his head. He was usually dressed in a black frock coat buttoned close to the chin, which gave him something of a clerical appearance. His health was always frail and this fact withdrew him somewhat from the world in general. Says one who knew him well: "He was a man of most exemplary character and life. He had no habits for which his admirers had to apologize. He lived as ever in his great Task-master's eye, nor was his name ever associated with any cause, business or enterprise which did not reflect back upon him all the dignity he conferred upon it."

It is not said that he made no mistakes or committed no errors of judgment. No one is infallible, and it has sometimes happened that the gravest mistakes, those fraught with the most terrible consequences, have been made by the best of men; but it *is* told of him with perfect truth that he was faithful to his highest convictions of right, and that he was never swayed from them by considerations of policy. He rightly deserves our reverence not only because he was the author of "one pure and good story the aim of which is to sow seeds of virtue," but because he was a man, and such men are not many, of whom it could with perfect truth be said — and though it was a simple thing it was a grand thing to say:

"*He had no habits for which his admirers had to apologize!*"

CHAPTER IX.

HANS CHRISTIAN ANDERSEN, "THE GOLDSMITH OF THE NORTH."

WASHINGTON IRVING wrote once of Oliver Goldsmith: "To be the most beloved of English writers, what a distinction, that, for a man!"

The story-teller of Copenhagen is perhaps dearer to the hearts of countless young readers than any other writer who ever lived. And what a distinction *that* is for any man to win!

Goldsmith and Andersen in certain important particulars were much alike. Both were simple and childlike in their natures; both were excessively vain — Goldsmith was as fond of fine clothes and as proud of appearing in them as any peacock of showing its plumage, and Andersen imagined himself the centre of everyone's thoughts — both were plain in feature even to positive ugliness, and both possessed a simplicity of literary style which goes directly to the hearts of their readers.

In regard to the vanity of these two men it should be said that it was of the most harmless character. Goldsmith never was envious of another's success, Andersen never let his self-esteem manifest itself in any way to the injury of another. The Danish writer was probably the most conceited man of his time, but it was a simple-hearted vanity which he could no more help, at least in later life, than a hen can help letting the whole poultry-yard know when she has laid an egg. For many years his was the most familiar figure in Copenhagen. Says one writer of Andersen: —

"High and low, rich and poor, he belonged to all. If he went out for a walk, everyone saluted him; if he visited the theater, all present welcomed him; children worshiped him, claimed him as belonging peculiarly to them; every household reserved for him a warm corner by the stove; not a family, from the king to the peasant, but had a knife and fork and a seat at the table ready for him."

It would be a rare nature indeed that such an amount of adulation would not affect, yet Andersen's sweetness of disposition was such that it did not make him arrogant or selfish; it simply distorted his vision and made him look at the world in general through the meshes of a net-work composed of the letters of his own name.

It must not, however, be imagined that because Andersen was so universally beloved by his countrymen that they regarded him as the greatest glory of their literature. On the contrary the Danes have always been puzzled to account for the admiration with which he is regarded in other lands to the neglect of several other Danish writers whom they rightfully regard as superior to him. But the reason is not so far to seek. The simplicity of his style made translation comparatively easy. English readers first made his acquaintance through the translations of his works by Mrs. Mary Howitt, herself a delightful writer for young people, and excellent Swedish and German versions appeared very early in his literary career. Then, too, people who made acquaintance with his works in their childhood have never been able to forget their love for the teller of fairy tales, and have regarded his novels with much the same feeling of uncritical admiration. To the majority of readers Andersen is the only Danish writer, a state of things as unfair to Denmark's other great authors as harmful to the fame of Andersen himself. But even when the just claims of his contemporaries have been satisfied much, very much, remains to be grateful for in the genius of Hans Andersen

He was born in Odense, the chief town on the Danish island of Funen, on April 2, 1805. His father was a shoemaker by trade, and a person of a melancholy disposition, a trait which at times showed itself in the character of his

famous son. Says Andersen in *The Story of My Life:*—

"During the first day of my existence my father is said to have sat by the bed and read aloud in Holberg, but I cried all the time. 'Wilt thou go to sleep, or listen quietly?' it is reported that my father asked in joke; but I still cried on; and even in the church, when I was taken to be baptized, I cried so loudly that the preacher, who was a passionate man, said, 'The younker screams like a cat!' which words my mother never forgot. A poor emigrant, Gomar, who stood as godfather, consoled her in the meantime by saying that the louder I cried as a child, all the more beautifully should I sing when I grew older."

The prophecy so early made was abundantly realized in later years. To the poor shoemaker's son was given a singing voice that has echoed round the world and gathered half the children in Christendom about his knees. It is pleasant to read of those early years in Odense. One of the very first events that he recalls is the visit of the Spaniards to Funen when he was but three years old. A Spanish soldier took him up in his arms, danced him on his knees and kissed him with tears in his eyes, mindful, no doubt, of some little Alfonso or Benita left behind in far-off Spain. Once when he was six years old he stood one evening with his mother and her neighbors in St. Knut's churchyard, gazing at the great comet which blazed its pathway across the sky, and the sight of which made a deep impression upon his childish mind. He writes thus of an incident of his childhood: —

"Sometimes during the harvest, my mother went into the field to glean. I accompanied her, and we went like Ruth in the Bible, to glean in the rich fields of Boaz. One day we went to a place the bailiff of which was well known for being a man of a rude and savage disposition. We saw him coming with a huge whip in his hand, and my mother and all the others ran away. I had wooden shoes on my bare feet, and in my haste I lost these and the thorns pricked me so that I could not run, and thus I was left behind and alone. The man came up and lifted his whip to strike me, when I looked him in the face and involuntarily exclaimed — 'How dare you strike me, when God can see it?'"

He was very young when he first went to the theater with his parents, and an odd figure the homely little fellow must have cut from his own account of himself: —

"As to my dress, I was rather spruce; an old woman altered my father's clothes for me; my mother would fasten three or four large pieces of silk with pins on my breast, and that had to do for vests; a large kerchief was tied round my neck with a mighty bow; my head was washed with soap and my hair curled, and then I was in all my glory. In that attire I went with my parents for the first time to the theater."

The first exclamation of the future poet and romancer on entering the theater was sufficiently prosaic, and was to the effect that if he had as many casks of butter at home as there were people in the theater that he could eat quantities of butter. His imagination was soon stimulated, however, and as he could go but seldom to the theater he procured a programme every day from the person who distributed the playbills, and seating himself in a corner would imagine a whole play from the title and list of characters.

Hans was still a mere lad when his father died, and after this event he was left much to himself while his mother went out washing in order to earn their living. He was fond of reading plays, and the more tragic they were the better. From reading plays he soon came to writing them and strange affairs they must have been. His first piece was a most doleful tragedy in which the entire *dramatis personæ* died miserably. This youthful effusion having met with adverse criticism from a neighbor he began a new piece in which a king and queen figured. He says : —

"I thought it not quite right that these dignified personages, as in Shakespeare, should speak like other men and women. I asked my mother and different people how a king ought properly to speak, but no one knew exactly. They said that it was so many years since a king had been in Odense, but that he certainly spoke in a foreign language. I procured myself, therefore, a sort of lexicon, in which were German, French and English words with Danish meanings, and this helped me. I took a word out of each language, and inserted them into the speeches of my king and queen. It was a regular Babel-like language, which I considered only suitable for such elevated personages. I desired now that everybody should hear my piece. It was a real felicity to me to read it aloud, and it never occurred to me that others should not have the same pleasure in listening to it."

The delight which the boy took in his crude fancies was the same sort of pleasure, with comparatively little modification, which the man afterwards took in his finished work. He was in some respects always a child, and he retained to the last the simplicity of heart which characterized his childhood and youth. He never grew old in feeling, but remained perennially young at heart. In the opening chapters of *The Story of My Life* we get many glimpses of his childhood as well as the continued account of his later years; but he put much of himself into his novels, and in *Only a Fiddler*, one may read the story of his longing for fame, his aspirations and his disappointments.

He was twenty-three when his first work of any importance appeared, entitled *A Pedestrian Journey from Holmen's Canal to Amack*. Holmen's Canal is one of the principal features of Copenhagen, and Amack or Amager is an island connected with the city by long bridges, so the journey in question was not a long one. The book which is mainly in rhyme and humorous in character, met with sudden and unexpected success and in consequence his confidence in his own powers could never afterwards be shaken. In 1829 a play of his called *Love on St. Nicholas's Tower* was acted with great success and the next year his first volume of poems appeared and became immediately popular. It was while on a journey through the Danish provinces in this year that he fell in love, and of this event we are told in the *Story of My Life*. His love was not returned and he cherished the memory of this, his only love episode, throughout his long life. In his next volume of poems, *Fancies and Sketches*, published soon after, we find many traces of this sorrow. His *Skyggebilleder*, or *Shadow-Pictures*, was his next book, a volume containing an account of his travels in the Hartz Mountains. A year or two later, in 1834, he published what must be reckoned, all things considered, his greatest work, the famous *Improvvisatore.* It is rarely that a man of one nationality enters so completely into the life of another people as does Andersen in this wonderful book. Madame de Staël ambitiously adds to her *Corinne* the sub-title "or Italy," but with far more truth might it be added to *The Improvvisatore.* The book *is* Italy. Northman as he was by birth, Andersen was Italian by temperament, and the fervor, the excitability, the enthusiasm, the longing to impart to others the details of one's own life so characteristic of Italians, and to a less extent of other nations of the south of Europe, were part of his very nature. No wonder, then, that he could enter so fully into the heart of Italian life as he does in the brilliant pages of the wonderful *Improvvisatore.*

It was the grown-up public for which he had written up to this time, but he was soon to gather about him another and much more extensive circle of readers, the children of Denmark at first, and later those of half the world. It was for these that he wrote in 1835 the first series of his *Eventyr* or *Fairy Tales* as we call them. The collection thus begun he added to from time to time during a long course of years. No writer of his time has surpassed Andersen in the ability to gain the attention of children by story-telling. The sweet simplicity of these tales never fails to win their admiration. Himself as guileless as a little child he saw very clearly into child nature and children know him for one of themselves.

Andersen's pen was very busy in these first years of authorship and, indeed, it was never long idle. In 1836 he gave to the world his novel called *O. T., or Life in Denmark*, as notable a picture of Danish life and customs as *The Improvvisatore*. The letters "O. T." were formerly branded on Danish criminals, and are the initials of the Odense Tughthuus, or House of Correction. In the same year his pastoral drama, *Parting and Meeting*, was acted on the stage with decided approval and in 1837 was published his novel *Only a Fiddler*. With Andersen's countrymen this is probably the most popular of any of his works and it is quite as faithful a picture of Danish life as *O. T.* The hero's father is the shoemaker of Odense, the melancholy father of Andersen himself, and the trials and sufferings of the talented Fiddler are drawn from events in Andersen's own life.

In 1839 he visited Sweden, and in his autobiography he tells us in an artless sort of way how he met with the once famous but now neglected Miss Bremer on board a steamboat in the course of his journey. While in Sweden he wrote a drama called *The Mulatto* which was so warmly applauded by the Swedes that he was invited to the university-city of Lund, where the students gave him a great banquet and a serenade. *A Picture Book without Pictures* was his next book, and in 1841 the results of a tour through Italy and Greece were embodied in *A Poet's Bazaar*, a book which met with greater favor abroad than at home. In 1846 the first part of his autobiography, *The Story of My Life*, was published, at subsequent periods continued to 1855, and then to the close of 1867. In this book it is easy enough to see the remarkable vanity of the man, but with this inordinate self-esteem was mingled so much of real gentleness and sweetness of temper that to judge harshly of Andersen because of his vanity becomes nearly impossible. Less popular than his other novels was the one entitled *The Two Baronesses*, his next work, but it is very well worth reading for its pictures of Danish life and its masterly delineation of character. In 1851 *Pictures of Sweden* appeared which by an English critic has been considered as his most delightful work, the autobiography excepted. It is certainly a fascinating book, though it hardly deserves the rank the critic mentioned accords it. During these years he was continually producing dramas many of which were exceedingly popular. One of these, called *Ole Lukoie*, was a sort of wonder-comedy in which the adventures of the dream-god, who figures in more than one of his fairy tales, were narrated. *A Poet's Day Dreams* was his next book. This appeared in 1853 and was followed at intervals of a few years by several collections of his *Wonder Stories*, and still later came the results of a Spanish tour called *In Spain*.

In 1873 his health began to fail and the end seemed not far off, yet he partially recovered and was seen again in the homes where he was always welcome. At last these visits had to be given up because his strength no longer admitted of his climbing the stairs that led to his friends' apartments. In the last winter of his life a young lad, the son of one of his friends, devoted himself to the care of the aged poet with an almost filial affection. When the weather permitted he would take him out for a daily walk, sustaining his feeble steps and guarding him from over-exertion in the tenderest manner, and when it was too cold for this the boy would sit by his friend cheering him with his bright boyish fancies or listening to some fairy tale that would never be written. Young Robert Henriques did in his own person what all young people whom the dear old man had loved and written for would gladly have done had the tender privilege been theirs.

April 2, 1875, was his seventieth birthday and deputations came from all parts of Denmark to greet him on that day; he was presented with a copy of one of his tales in thirty-two languages, money was raised to erect his statue in Copenhagen and to build a home for poor children which should bear his name, and on the little house in Odense where he was born was placed a tablet with his name and the date of his birth. He never appeared in public after this and four months later, on the fourth of August, 1875, he entered into rest.

On the day of his funeral all the city shops were closed and Copenhagen was draped in mourning. The Church of Our Lady was filled with those who had loved him. On the coffin were heaped flowers, laurels and palms, and near it stood a great company of children strewing flowers. Close by, too, stood the King with his eldest son and Prince John of Glücksburg, bareheaded and in their regal robes. In his simple, artless way the dead poet had loved pomp and beauty all his life and so at his funeral all the magnificence and ceremony that he would have delighted in were not wanting. Just at the hour of noon the great organ began a tender prelude and then that vast company, king and peasant, rich and poor, sang Andersen's own hymn, "Like to the Leaf which Falleth from the Tree." Then Dean Rothe recited one of Andersen's last poems and spoke earnestly and tenderly of the man whom all Denmark had delighted to honor and was followed by the aged bishop of Odense, who said the farewell from the birthplace of Andersen. After this Carl Plough's poem, "Sleep, Weary Child," written for the occasion, was sung and Andersen's friend, the composer Hartmann, played on the organ the music he had written long before for the funeral of Thorwaldsen. As the music trembled into silence people from all parts of the church went up to the chancel and laid wreaths and flowers upon the coffin. In the centre of these tributes lay a palm branch and wreath from Odense, the city of his birth, the scene of his early struggles. When the last wreath had been brought the coffin was borne down the centre aisle by a number of students followed by the various delegations from all parts of Denmark bearing crape-bordered banners, and a long procession of mourning friends. All along the route to the cemetery people sat at their windows clad in deep mourning and many of the houses and all the shipping in the harbor had flags at half-mast. As the procession left the church great numbers of poor people hastened into the building to gather the leaves and flowers which had fallen from his coffin and even the smallest leaf was lovingly cherished.

In spite of his love for splendor and show he never became forgetful of his own poor estate in early youth or ceased to have the warmest sympathy with the humblest person. His vanity, his self-esteem were in him the most amiable of foibles, the heart beneath was one of the tenderest and gentlest that ever beat. On a laurel wreath from Berlin which lay upon his coffin was fastened this inscription, as touching as it is full of tender truth: —

"Thou art not dead, though thine eyes are closed.
In children's hearts thou shalt live forever."

CHAPTER X.

DANIEL DEFOE.

IN the winter of 1711–12 all London was very busy talking about a certain man who had recently returned from a voyage to the Southern Seas. At the coffee-houses the men about town conversed of him with Addison and Steele and the other literary men of the day. Fine ladies in their sedan-chairs going to and from the play were full of the topic, and even the linkboys who stood without the doors of the playhouse till the acting should be over discussed it with the waiting chairmen. Hosts of people visited the sailor, whose name was Alexander Selkirk, and listened to his account of the solitary life he led for four years upon the island of Juan Fernandez. After a time several accounts of

Selkirk's adventures appeared in print, then fresher topics came to the surface and so this nine days wonder passed from mind.

Several attempts, it is true, were made to use it as literary material, but they failed and it seemed as if Selkirk and his narrative had made no lasting impression upon the age. But nevertheless one man of genius had kept the affair in mind, and in 1719 this Selkirk germ flowered into the immortal *Robinson Crusoe*. Its author was perhaps the one man of his time who could develop such a tale as *Robinson Crusoe* from the outline furnished by Selkirk's adventures. He possessed in a remarkable degree the gift of circumstantial narration — the power, that is, of inventing a series of facts which shall seem perfectly natural, and the ability to throw over these facts, no matter how extraordinary in themselves, a wonderful air of reality. Among his contemporaries were men of greater gifts than he, but no one but Defoe, it is safe to say, could at that time have written a romance like this.

It is not a very clear notion that we get of Daniel Defoe from the works of his contemporaries or from the writers of our own day. An accomplished essayist writing thirty years ago calls him a "model of integrity," and a more recent writer says, " He was a great, truly great liar, perhaps the greatest liar that ever lived." Of these two estimates the latter is perhaps nearest the truth.

He was born in London in 1661, the son of a butcher in the parish of Cripplegate, named Foe. When he was about forty he changed his signature from " D. Foe " to " Defoe," and seems after that period to have written his name " Daniel De Foe " or " Daniel Defoe " as it pleased him. In 1731 he died in Moorfields, London, accomplishing in his life of seventy years a vast amount of literary work, more in quantity than any man of his time, busy as some of them were.

The list of his writings includes two hundred and ten works, ranging over the greatest variety of topics, and yet authorship was by no means

DANIEL DEFOE.

his only claim to notice in his time. He was an active politician throughout his life and was manufacturer, merchant and journalist by turns. He was originally intended for the ministry, but after completing the course of training for that purpose abandoned the idea of that profession, a fortunate decision, for his talents, however great, were not those best fitted for exercise in the pulpit. In 1685 he became a hose merchant, but his success in this business may be guessed from the fact that seven years later he was obliged to flee from his creditors. Tradition states that he went to Bristol and was there called the "Sunday Gentleman" from his appearing in public only on that day, for fear of the bailiffs kept him indoors the rest of the week. Later on we hear of him in various occupations, among others that of the manufacture of bricks, and it is pleasant to read that he labored diligently to pay his creditors.

In 1697 his first important work was published, entitled *An Argument Showing that a*

Standing Army with Consent of Parliament is not Inconsistent with a Free Government. The title may not sound attractive to us now, but the book was very effective in its day, and is a marvel of direct and vivacious reasoning. From this time forward he used his pen vigorously upon all the foremost topics of the period, and when he wrote *The True-Born Englishman* he became suddenly famous. It appeared near the end of King William's reign, at a time when the king was exceedingly unpopular and the dislike of foreigners was at its height. Defoe in this satire declared that no such thing as a true-born Englishman existed, that they were all descended from foreigners. One would naturally imagine a turbulent London mob would have hung the audacious author before his own door. But they did nothing of the kind. The witty, hard-hitting strokes of his satire tickled the English sense of humor and eighty thousand copies of the pamphlet were sold in London streets. A still more famous political work of his entitled *The Shortest Way with Dissenters* appeared in 1703. Never was a jest taken so seriously, or a whole nation so completely "sold" as we should now say. In this work the author satirically urged that if all persons attending non-conformist chapels should be banished from the country, and all non-conformist preachers hanged, the evil of Dissent would be ended forever. Extreme as these measures of the clever writer seem, and in the urging of which he was only satirizing the intolerance of churchmen, they for a time much delighted the High Churchmen; but when these discovered that they had been tricked their rage knew no bounds. For a time Defoe concealed himself, but that the printer and publisher should not suffer in his stead he surrendered himself. The House of Commons ordered his book burned by the common hangman, and at his trial he was condemned to pay a large fine to the Crown, to stand three times in the pillory, be imprisoned during the Queen's good pleasure, and find sureties for his good behavior for seven years.

In the State of Delaware the pillory is still occasionally used, and one may sometimes see there a culprit undergoing that most unpleasant kind of punishment. But the shame of such a punishment lies in its desert, and Defoe had done nothing to deserve his sentence. For three days the most popular Englishman of the period stood there in the pillory about which gathered the multitude who covered the pillory platform with flowers, while barrels of ale and wine were drunk in his honor by his enthusiastic admirers. He remained in prison till August, 1703; but various works of his were sent to the press from there, and the time was by no means lost. It would be impossible to detail here a tenth part of Defoe's adventures. His restless nature was ever impelling him into controversy and intrigue. To most remarkable powers of argument and wonderful skill as a satirist he united an unscrupulous disposition and a confidence in his ability to extricate himself from any complications into which his activity might plunge him — a confidence, it must be confessed, not unsupported by experience.

Our modern habit of close investigation is fast disposing of the literary anecdotes which are often told in connection with authors. For instance, it used to be asserted that a certain London bookseller having on his shelves a large number of copies of a very dull book by Drelincourt, called *The Fear of Death,* induced Defoe to write a "puff" for this volume and that the *True Relation of the Apparition of One Mrs. Veal* was the result, and that *The Fear of Death* accordingly rapidly disappeared from the bookseller's shop. The reason for the sudden demand for the book consisted in the fact that the ghostly Mrs. Veal earnestly recommended the perusal of the work. Alas for the facts! If the inventor of this tale had had the fear of lying before his eyes, he would have told us that Defoe's book was first published without any reference to *The Fear of Death,* which was already popular and needed no "puffing" of this sort.

But as " error runs a mile while truth is putting on his boots " this anecdote is likely to survive as long as the world cares to listen about Defoe. And that will be for centuries to come, for as the author of *Robinson Crusoe* his hold upon the hearts of young people is perhaps greater than that of any other writer.

It is with Defoe that the art of novel-writing really begins. Fiction, in prose at least, was new to the world then, and the reading public were eager to read *Moll Flanders*, *Captain Singleton*, and the other romances which Defoe rapidly gave to the world. It is not easy to think of a period when people found themselves reading novels for the first time. The sensations of a child old enough to think about the matter who tastes candy for the first time in his life can fitly be compared to the feelings of the first novel-readers. These books of Defoe's are not such as we should enjoy now, for they are coarse in tone and deal with customs and manners to which we are now fortunately strangers;

but they show his wonderful power of story-telling, a power which reaches its height in *Robinson Crusoe*.

"Homely plain writing," Defoe termed his style, but it is this "homely" directness of his that constitutes the charm of *Robinson Crusoe*. It was written in the full maturity of his powers, for he was fifty-eight years old at the time, and all the bent of his life was such as to fit him for this sort of writing. Few men could make fiction seem more like fact than he. His whole career was such as to create a general belief that he was untrustworthy; yet he could pass himself off with the Tories as a Tory, and with the Whigs as a Whig, while he was constantly appearing before the public in assumed characters. Now while all this is by no means to his credit, it does show his inventive spirit in a very strong light, and how he was able by the exercise of this faculty to throw around the simple story of a man living on a desert island such a wonderful air of reality. When we read *Robin-*

son Crusoe we feel that the hero would not naturally have acted in any other way than he actually did. And it is this fact which gives its life to the book. Defoe might have kept his inventive powers in their place and never have gained his reputation for untrustworthiness, and still have given *Robinson Crusoe* to the world as perfect as it is now, no doubt, but we must look at facts as they are and not as we should wish them to be. And the fact is that this immortal story-teller was a man to whom the truth was a stranger. He was seldom straightforward. He was fertile in expedients to pass off falsehood for truth, and it is this gift of invention which, rightfully exercised in *Robinson Crusoe*, made, when carried into actual practice in life, so untrustworthy a character as his.

Says one biographer: —

"If he is judged by the measures that he labored for, and not by the means that he employed, few Englishmen have lived more deserving of their country's gratitude. He may have been self-seeking and vain-glorious, but in his political life self-seeking and vain-glory were elevated by their alliance with higher and wider aims."

And with this judgment we leave him, remembering always that if he were lacking in integrity of purpose he could nevertheless serve his countrymen nobly, and that in spite of all his faults he was great enough to write for his time, and for all time, *Robinson Crusoe.*

CHAPTER XI.

LA MOTTE FOUQUE "THE VALIANT."

SEVENTY years ago one of the most popular names in German literature was that of an author whose French surname strikes one somewhat oddly in a list of German authors. Once the works of Friedrich Heinrich Karl Fouqué, Baron de la Motte, were among the treasures of every German household, and whenever a forthcoming volume of his was announced the libraries were besieged with applications for it. But long before his death the high tide of popularity had subsided and with it ebbed the taste for the romantic school of composition of which he was one of the great masters; yet one work of his has become a classic and is likely to live on.

Nearly a century before his birth the revocation of the Edict of Nantes had driven his family from France. They sought refuge in Holland, and Fouqué's grandfather having entered the Prussian army, the family became citizens of Prussia at a later period. His grandfather, also named Friedrich, rose to distinction in the Prussian service and was honored with the precarious friendship of Frederick the Great. Being a person of rare prudence he succeeded in avoiding all the sunken rocks and dangerous shallows in the stream of courtly favor and his friendly relations with the choleric monarch continued unbroken throughout his life.

His son entered the Prussian service likewise, at one time being an officer of dragoons, and it was while he was living at Brandenburg on the Havel, not then being in active service, that his son Friedrich was born, on the twelfth of February, 1777. The family admiration for the monarch was so great that the child was named, not unnaturally, for the illustrious emperor who stood sponsor for him at his baptism. His earliest years were spent on his father's estate at Sacro, near Potsdam, and later at Lentzke, not far distant. He was an only child and much pains was taken with his education which was conducted at home under various tutors, one of whom, the author August Hülse, encouraged in every way the dawning literary tastes of the boy.

It was not exactly a lonely life that he spent at Lentzke, but it seems to have been somewhat monotonous. Still there were certain events in it to look forward to, or to recall when they were once past; for his holidays were almost always spent with relatives who lived in a delightfully romantic old castle near Halle, a circumstance which no doubt strengthened his inborn love of the romantic side of life and literature. Sometimes, too, there were visits to Potsdam from which the boy would return wild with enthusiasm for the great Frederick whom he had seen and who perhaps had given him a kind word or two or patted his godson's head.

The sound of military music and the sight of

LA MOTTE FOUQUE.

the soldiers had their due share in fostering the military spirit in this son and grandson of a soldier and the prospect of pursuing the study of law at the University of Halle grew less and less alluring. At last he gave up the design of doing so altogether, and in 1794 entered the army as *übercompleter Cornet* in the service of the Grand Duke of Weimar, and when only nineteen served in the fatal campaign of the Rhine. For several years after this he led a semi-military life with his regiment, but was not in active service.

He married early, but the marriage was not a fortunate one, and a divorce took place. In 1802, when but twenty-five, he married again, the lady being the Frau von Rochow, who as Caroline, Baroness de la Motte Fouqué, became an author of note whose books still find a place in libraries.

About this time he procured his discharge from the army and devoted himself to a literary career which was to last for forty years. His first work, *Dramatische Spiele*, was published by the famous brothers Schlegel in 1804. The friendship of the Schlegels, particularly that of August Wilhelm, was of great benefit to the young writer. By the latter he was induced to study Spanish poetry, a pursuit quite in harmony with Fouqué's romantic vein. This initial work was soon followed by *Romanzen aus dem Thal Ronceval*, the first fruits of the Schlegel influence, and by two plays, the *Falk* and the *Reh*. Much encouraged by the discriminating praise of the Schlegels Fouqué continued vigorously at work, producing in 1806 a metrical version of an old prose romance, the *Historie vom edlem Ritter Galmy*, and the poem *Schiller's Todtenfeir* which latter was written in conjunction with Bernhardin. In 1808 came the romance called *Alvin*, which brought him many literary admirers, among whom was his contemporary, Jean Paul Richter, who styled him "*Der Tapfere*" or "The Valiant." In the same year, too, was published his *Sigurd der Schlangentödter*, the first of his books appearing with his name, the others having been published under the pseudonym "Pellegrin." He continued writing and publishing at frequent intervals up to the year 1814, when among other pieces of literary work he produced his famous *Jahreszciten*, a series in four parts, the spring number consisting of his famous romance *Undine*, the summer number containing *Die Beiden, Hauptleute*, the autumn division *Aslauga's Ritter* and *Algin und Jucunda* and the winter division, *Sintram und seine Gefährten*.

In the midst of this active literary career he had in 1813 returned to the army and at the battle of Lüzten he twice narrowly escaped with his life. In the night after the battle he was entrusted with the carrying of an important dispatch and while in the discharge of this duty his horse stumbled in deep water and threw him. From this accident an illness resulted which disabled him from military service. He accordingly received an honorable discharge, was presented with the decoration of the " Johannterorden" or cross of the Order of St. John, and was raised to the rank of major of cavalry. He now returned to his home at Neunhausen with his wife and daughter, and once more resumed his pen.

The list of his works published after this date is a long one, but they are quite forgotten now for the most part, and slumber quietly on library shelves. In 1831 his wife died and removing to Halle he married there for the third time. Here his last years were peacefully spent in writing and in lecturing at the university on the history of poetry, and having gone to Berlin in 1843 for the purpose of delivering his lectures in that city as well, he died there quite suddenly, January 23.

His was a well-filled life, but the highest measure of his achievement was reached when he was yet a comparatively young writer, when in 1814 the exquisite romance *Undine* was given to the world. The same year witnessed the appearance of a story of chivalry which Fouqué considered one of his most successful works, *Die Fahrten Thiodolf des Isländers*, but the judgment of posterity has not confirmed its author's estimate. Of all his many books only the chivalric romance *Der Zauberring* published in 1811 and *Jahreszaten*, which contains the famous *Undine* survive. These, particularly the latter, have weathered the fluctuations of popular taste and have become so integral a part of the literature and the thought of the time that they cannot readily be displaced. And after all only the very greatest authors go down to posterity with more than a book or two under the arm. Sometimes the book is a very small one, sometimes it is reduced to a few pages, a single leaf even, but the literary immortality that depends upon but a single leaf is often as sure as that of a Homer or a Cicero.

That the greater part of Fouqué's work was so soon consigned to neglect was owing to the fact that he had so slight a hold upon the life of his time. He was not a deep thinker or a man of highly-wrought feelings. The problems of modern life except as viewed occasionally from a military standpoint had little attraction for him and he failed to grasp them in any adequate measure, and the coldness of his temperament effectually prevented him from putting any great amount of passion into his romances. The romantic school of literature of which, following the lead of the brothers Schlegel, he was so eminent a representative, appeals mainly to the fancy and the imagination and has almost no power over the emotions. The distinguishing characteristic of Fouqué's mind seems to have been the attempt to present an ideal of Christian knighthood. In some form or other this ideal appears uppermost in his fancy in nearly all his works reaching his apotheosis in *Undine* and *Aslauga's Ritter*. A very just estimate of his character in this respect is made by Carlyle who says:—

"A pure, sensitive heart, deeply reverent of truth and beauty and heroic virtue, a quick perception of certain forms embodying these high qualities, and a delicate and dainty hand in picturing them forth are gifts which few readers of his works will contest him. At the same time, it must be granted, he has no preëminence, either of head or heart, and his circle of activity, though full of animation, is far from comprehensive. He is, as it were, possessed by one idea. A few notes, some of them in truth, of rich melody, yet still a very few, include the whole music of his being. The Chapel and the Tilt-yard stand in the background or the foreground, in all the scenes of his universe. He gives us knights, soft-hearted and strong-armed; full of Christian self-denial, patience, meekness, and gay, easy daring; they stand before us in their mild frankness, with suitable equipment, and accompaniment of squire and dame, and frequently the whole has a true, though seldom a vigorous, poetic life. If this can content us, it is well; if not, there is no help; for change of scene and person brings little change of subject; even when no chivalry is mentioned, we feel too clearly the influence of its unseen presence. Nor can it be said that in this solitary department his success is of the very highest sort. To body forth the spirit of Christian knighthood in existing poetic forms, to wed that old *sentiment* to modern *thoughts* was a task which he could not attempt. He has turned rather to the fictions and machinery of former days, and transplanted his heroes into distant ages and scenes divided by their nature from our common world. Their manner of existence comes imaged back to us faint and ineffectual, like the crescent of the setting moon.

These things, however, are not faults, but the want of merits. Where something is effected, it were ungracious to reckon up too narrowly how much is left untried. In all his writings Fouqué shows himself as a man deeply imbued with feelings of religion, honor and brotherly love; he sings of faith and affection with a full heart; and a spirit of tenderness, and vestal purity, and meek heroism sheds salutary influences from his presence. He is no primate or bishop in the Church Poetical; but a simple chaplain, who merits the honors of a small but well-discharged function, and claims no other."

There are few things in the German language more beautiful than the sweet simplicity of Fouqué's style. "Exquisite" is the word which must be used to describe it and no reader of *Undine* or *Aslauga's Ritter* will care to apply to it any other term. Its airy grace is inimitable. Says one of his critics:—

"Fouqué aimed at ethereal beauty, delighted in word-painting, and flitted continually between the glories of a crimson Spanish sunset and the cold steel-blue of a north German nightfall."

Very few of Fouqué's writings have been translated into English. *Undine* and *Sintram* have, it is true, and more than once; and the *Zauberring* and *Aslauga's Ritter* have appeared in an English dress; but these are all and for the reasons already named it is not likely that the list of translations will be increased.

Aslauga's Ritter has found fewer readers than *Undine*. Aslauga, it will be remembered by readers of the *Nibelungen Lied*, was the daughter of Siegfried and Brynhild, and in this romance, long after she had ended her days as the wife of the Danish king Ragnar Lodbrog, she appears to the Knight Froda and becomes the inspiration of his life. A passage from Carlyle's translation of the tale will give some idea of the style of this charming romance: —

"But Edwald continued dreaming, dreaming; and many other visions passed before him, all of a lovely cast, though he could not recollect them, when far in the morning he opened his smiling eyes. Froda and his mysterious song alone stood clear before his memory. He now saw well that his friend was dead but he sorrowed not because of it in his mind, feeling as he did, that the pure heart of the hero and singer could nowhere find its proper joy, save in the Land of Light, in blissful communion with the high spirits of the ancient time. He glided softly from his sleeping Hildegardis into the chamber of the departed. He was lying on his bed of rest, almost as beautiful as he had looked in the vision; and the gold helmet on his head was entwisted in a wondrous, beaming lock of hair. Then Edwald made a fair shady grave on consecrated ground, summoned the castle chaplain, and with his help interred in it his heroic Froda." *

* For a very beautiful version of the story of Aslang, the reader must turn to *The Fostering of Aslang* in William Morris's *Earthly Paradise*.

CHAPTER XII.

THE AUTHOR OF "PAUL AND VIRGINIA."

WHEN by chance we hear the name of Elsinore what other name comes at once to our thoughts like an echo of the first? What name but Hamlet! With Verona are linked forever in our memories the names of Juliet and Romeo. Grand Pré and Acadie summon recollections of Evangeline and Gabriel. Westward of Chili, far out in the Pacific, lies an island visited by few but familiarly known the world over because along its sands and through its woods once roamed Robinson Crusoe. In the Indian Ocean lies another island, once owning allegiance to Holland, then to France, and now to England — the island of Mauritius or Isle de France, which is dear to hundreds of thousands of hearts simply because it was once the home of Paul and Virginia.

Yet none of these people had ever an actual existence. They never breathed our air, never lived and never died, but yet they are more real to us than nine tenths of the people we meet upon our daily walks, more real than those whose names crowd the pages of history. And they will be just as real, just as actual personalities far down the centuries to come as they are to us of the present one. They are part of our individual life and they are part of the world's life also.

Do you ask why this is so? Simply because these men and women stand for vital, enduring facts which the world recognizes as such. Every one perceives in the person of Hamlet the struggle that is eternally going on in souls that acknowledge a duty before them and who lack decision of character to perform it without hesitation. Robinson Crusoe and his adventures represent the age-long struggle of man

JACQUES-HENRI-BERNARDIN DE ST. PIERRE.

with circumstances. Disappointed and unhappy but ever-faithful love sees itself reflected in the story of the Veronese lovers, or those of Acadie, or of far-distant Mauritius. It is because these people of the imagination in one sense are in another sense not creatures of the imagination at all, but people of the past and of the future as well as of the present, since they represent some of the springs of action in human character, that they are so real to us. They do exist as truly as ever Queen Elizabeth or Cromwell did, and Elsinore, Grand Pré, Verona, Juan Fernandez and Mauritius are not more real than they.

In the *salon* of Madame Necker in Paris there was gathered upon one occasion, one hundred years ago, a brilliant company of literary people to listen to the reading of a romance entitled *Paul and Virginia* by the author, one Jacques-Henri-Bernardin de St. Pierre. As the reading proceeded the attention of the listeners flagged, some of them whispered to each other and looked at their watches, those near the door stole out, and one or two either went to sleep or pretended to do so. Some of the ladies wept over the sorrowful conclusion, but as no word of praise was heard at the end of the reading they did not dare to confess that they had been interested. Who can blame the author if he left the *salon* in the deepest depression believing that his literary sentence-of-death had been pronounced?

He had up to this time published no book, but had for many years devoted himself to the preparation of a work called *Arcadia*, and it is from the materials gathered for this that *The Studies of Nature, Paul and Virginia* and *The Indian Cottage* were written. But the result of the reading at Madame Necker's was a blow to his literary ambition, and but for a fortunate accident *Paul and Virginia*, incomparably the best of his works, might never have seen the public eye.

Among the friends of St. Pierre was Horace

Vernet, the celebrated artist. Visiting his friend one day in the humble quarters which St. Pierre then occupied, he found him sunk in despair, for the disastrous scene at Madame Necker's was never out of his mind. Vernet inquired the cause of his friend's grief, and when told asked to have the narrative read to him. That St. Pierre was loth to undertake a second reading of the unlucky manuscript can well be believed, but his reluctance yielded to the other's persistence, and he began. Vernet's mood of critical attention soon gave way to one of unrestrained delight, and when the reading was finished he rose and embraced his friend, exclaiming enthusiastically, "Happy genius! you have produced a *chef-d'œuvre!* My friend, you are a great painter and I dare promise you a splendid reputation."

The effect of this warm praise upon St. Pierre's drooping spirits was to give him confidence in his own powers. By and by he took courage and printed his *Paul and Virginia* and became at once one of the foremost literary men of his time. He had been long in winning distinction, but it was substantial fame when it came at last. He was of respectable but not noble origin, and was born at Havre on January 19, 1737, so that when he become famous he was more than forty years old.

As a boy St. Pierre was noted for his affectionate, loving disposition and his fondness for animals. On one occasion his father pointed out to him the lofty towers of the cathedral of Rouen. The boy gazed earnestly upwards and his father, wishing to see how the sight would impress a child, asked what he thought of them. But Henri had eyes only for the swallows circling round the spires, and exclaimed, "*Mon Dieu! qu'elles volent haut!*" "How high they fly!"—a reply which seems greatly to have disappointed his father who looked for a very different response.

A prominent trait in his character was his impulse always to side with the oppressed, and any form of suffering roused his sympathies instantly. When he was very young he read with eager interest the *Lives of the Saints* and once concluded he would be a hermit like some of the saintly heroes of whom he had read. Accordingly he took a lunch with him into the woods, expecting as soon as his earthly sustenance was exhausted that angels would appear with further supplies. Evening came, but not the angels, and the arrival of his nurse who found him asleep at the foot of a tree cut short an experiment that might have sorely tested his faith.

Something of this same simplicity of faith that led him to make the attempt just narrated remained with him all his life. In a century dominated by scepticism, and amongst a people who held their religious beliefs very lightly, he was conspicuous for the depth and sincerity of his faith. But his faith was of the heart and not of the head; it was founded upon sentiment and not upon reflection. This simplicity and singleness of intent, however admirable in itself, led him into a maze of contradictions and absurdities when he attempted to explain the purposes of natural phenomena. He asks in one place in his *Etudes de la Nature:* —

"Why do some trees shed their leaves and others do not? It is difficult to explain the cause but easy to recognize the purpose. If the birch and the larch of the north cast their leaves at the approach of winter, it is to furnish a bedding for the beasts of the forests; and if the cone-like fir-tree preserves its foliage all the year, it is to furnish the same beasts with shelter amid the snows."

Regarding this extraordinary statement, a critic says: —

"Shelter and bedding at once, it is evident, would have been too good for these poor animals; so it is arranged that their bedding shall be under bare trees, and shall all be covered up by snow, when the time comes for them to fly to the hospitable shelter of the evergreens. Again he tells us that the reason why cocoanuts grow on high trees is that by the noise of their fall they may attract the animals whom they furnish with food. It apparently did not occur to him that the cocoanut on the ground was quite as visible an object as the acorn, which also serves various animals for food, and yet falls without noise. . . It makes no difference to M. de St. Pierre how many different constructions any established order of things may be capable of bearing, so long as there is one out of them all that suits his purpose is quite enough to prove that it alone is the true interpretation of the phenomena. Thus, on the same page, he tells with admiration how some trees are so fenced round with thorns that the birds who lodge in them are protected from all attacks from below, and how other trees, that are fenced round in the same way, have long rope-like growths depending from their branches, so that monkeys and other animals that devour birds' eggs can climb up and take the citadel by surprise. So whether the birds escape their adversaries, or whether they fall a prey to them, there is equal reason to admire the wonderful designs of the Creator, who is now on the side of the birds and now on that of the monkeys."

The unscientific temper of his mind and his inability to see more than one aspect of the case at a time of course renders his conclusions of little value in many instances; but his disposition to see good in everything, though carried by him to illogical extremes, had its root in the best principles of human nature, and was as conspicuous in his childhood as in his later years.

At the age of twelve he read *Robinson Crusoe* and was immediately filled with a wild desire to have an island of his own and establish a society. As years went on this desire deepened. At the Jesuit college in Caen, at Martinique, where he went with his uncle, as a lieutenant in Germany, and at Malta, the notion was still in his mind and at the age of twenty-six he set out for Russia to ask Catherine II. for a grant of land near the Caspian Sea where he might carry out his theories. But as might have been expected he received no encouragement at the Russian Court and the project which had been so long cherished was at length reluctantly abandoned.

At the age of thirty he returned to France, and after the lapse of a year was offered the position of engineer to an expedition to the Isle of France, and Madagascar, which he accepted. Always ready to believe the best of those with whom he came in contact St. Pierre gave a ready ear to those who told him that now he would have the chance to carry out his benevolent theories in founding a community in Madagascar. Hardly had the expedition sailed when he ascertained that it was practically a slave-hunting affair and the people concerned in it very far from being those upon whose assistance he could count. The disappointment was a severe one, but its effects were lasting; he indulged in no more dreams of founding Utopias. He left his uncongenial companions when he reached the Isle of France and remained there a resident of the island for more than two years. During this time he devoted himself to the study of natural history, and possibly the outlines of the story of *Paul and Virginia* were shaping themselves in his mind during that time. Some of the results of his life here were made public on his return to his native country in his book called *Voyage to the Isle of France*. It met with some attention and the *Etudes de la Nature* was even better received; but as before stated it was the publication of

Paul and Virginia which made him famous. The world at once reversed the contemptuous judgment which the frequenters of the Necker *salon* had passed upon the tale, and at the end of a century its verdict remains practically unchanged.

A striking instance of St. Pierre's independence of character was shown in 1798 when at a meeting of the Moral Science department of the *Institut* he appended to a report which he read before it a strong avowal of his own belief in God. Hardly had the assembly become aware of his line of argument when the members burst forth with exclamations of rage and derision. Nearly all his hearers were atheists, and his words at once aroused the most vehement opposition. They scoffed at his age, ridiculed what they called his superstition, and some even challenged him to a duel. Vainly St. Pierre endeavored to make himself heard, and at last when one of the members cried out " I swear there is no God and I demand that his name never again be pronounced within these walls!" he retired from the disorderly assembly. As to the fitness of time and place for making his avowal, there is room for difference of opinion; but in regard to his courage and independence in so doing there can be no question.

If St. Pierre's earlier years were full of vicissitudes and anxieties, the latter half of his life was peaceful and happy. Rather late in life he married M'lle Didot and became the father of two children whom he named Paul and Virginia. To them he thus tenderly refers in his *Harmonies of Nature:* —

"When I was unmarried and when I published the first volume of my *Studies of Nature*, I said in that work, without suspecting that there would be any truth in my prophecy, that 'the next generation would in some respect belong to me.' This was meant to apply only to those improvements in education with which I was then occupied; but I have had my wishes fulfilled in other respects, for I can hardly go into a public walk without hearing mothers or nurses, brothers or sisters, call children by the name of Paul and Virginia. I often turn unconsciously around and imagine for the moment that these are my children, for I also have a Virginia and a Paul, who form a crown of roses for my gray hairs. I embrace accordingly the opportunity of using their names with the greater pleasure, as it will enable me to exhibit a sketch of their opening dispositions. My Virginia is now five years old, and will soon become capable of understanding such lessons; my Paul is an infant scarcely twelve months old, but he discovers the mildest disposition, and the warmest affection for his little sister."

Some time after the death of the mother of his children, St. Pierre married again and this second marriage appears to have been as fortunate as the first. The last years of his life seem indeed to have been exceptionally happy. His young wife was devoted to him, in his children he took constant delight, and the income from his works, to which a Government pension was now added, enabled him to live at ease and minister to the wants of others. The vexations and trials of his youth were now far in the past and his old age was a calm and peaceful one. He had just passed his seventy-eighth birthday when on the twenty-first of January, 1814, his serene old age was merged into another life.

We may smile at his early follies, his absurdities, his simplicities, but it is a kindly smile, a smile where no trace of a sneer can linger. All his long life he retained a childlike singleness of temper and gentleness and when the final summons came, "Lo! he whose heart was even as a little child's, answered to his name and stood in the presence of the Master."

www.ingramcontent.com/pod-product-compliance
Lightning Source LLC
Chambersburg PA
CBHW020906230426
43666CB00008B/1333